What Makes You Grateful?

Voices from Around the World

Compiled by

Anne O. Kubitsky

(AOK)

skirt!

Guilford, Connecticut
An imprint of Globe Pequot Press

To buy books in quantity for corporate use
or incentives, call **(800) 962-0973**
or e-mail **premiums@GlobePequot.com**.

 skirt!® is an attitude . . . spirited, independent, outspoken, serious, playful and irreverent, sometimes controversial, always passionate.

skirt!® is an imprint of Globe Pequot Press.
skirt!® is a registered trademark of Morris Publishing Group, LLC, and is used with express permission.

Library of Congress Cataloging-in-Publication Data

What makes you grateful? : voices from around the world / [compiled by]
Anne O. Kubitsky.
     pages cm
 Includes bibliographical references and index.
 ISBN 978-0-7627-8671-8 (alk. paper)
1. Gratitude. I. Kubitsky, Anne O., editor of compilation.
 BF575.G68W43 2013
 179'.9—dc23

                                                                2013026844

Printed in the United States of America

10 9 8 7 6 5 4 3

This book is dedicated to my parents, Diana, Sean,
and all the wonderful people who continue to participate in this project.
Thank you for inspiring me to look for the good.

—AOK

To speak gratitude is courteous and pleasant,
to enact gratitude is generous and noble,
but to live gratitude is to touch Heaven.
—Johannes A. Gaertner

Table of Contents

WHAT MAKES YOU GRATEFUL?

You are invited to share a glimmer of gladness in a community art project.

Simply:
1. Take this postcard(s)
2. Write/draw/paint/glue something that you're grateful for
3. Stamp and mail your card

Just make sure it's concise, legible, and can make it through the post.

To view the online gallery, visit:
www.lookforthegoodproject.org

What I'm Grateful For
PO Box 602
Old Lyme, CT 06371
USA

The Look for the Good Project

It started innocently enough. On a whim—one crisp, fall day in October of 2011—I printed 500 invitation cards asking people to share a glimmer of gladness on a postcard and distributed them in post offices, parks, cafes, community centers, libraries, and anywhere I went. I thought it might be fun and wondered if anyone would write back. And to my delight, people did. Within three weeks I was getting handmade postcard responses from Connecticut, Massachusetts, Texas, Oregon, Washington, Alaska, Germany, Australia . . . and now, two years later, I have thousands of responses from all over the world—letters, e-mails, postcards, text messages, phone calls, music, and art of all kinds. In fact, I got so many responses that I've hosted a number of exhibits, shared the cards online and in the media, and I unexpectedly went through a lot of healing.

You see, about twelve years before this project began, I went through a traumatic sexual assault that I never fully processed. Still in my teens, I found the experience so upsetting that I bottled it up for the next decade, hiding behind philosophy and science to distance myself from the pain. In fact, I couldn't even remember the whole thing until just a few years ago. That's why these postcards have been so healing.

Little by little, postcard by postcard, I began to see that I wasn't alone. We *all* have bad things that happen to us. We each have something we regret. But the question is: What do you do about it? Do you get stuck in the drama of the experience and use it as an excuse to stay angry and afraid? Or do you use it as an opportunity to learn a little more about life, love, peace, happiness, and all the intangible qualities that make life great? That's what this project is helping me do—learn. And I hope that's what it does for you, too. Because there's *always something* to be grateful for. We just have to be open enough to see it.

For example, to keep this project going, I had to consolidate my expenses—selling all my stuff and giving up my apartment. I lived in a small space on the second floor of a beautiful old house overlooking the Connecticut River. Raspberries grew along the wooded paths, deer frequented the neighborhood, I could bicycle to the farmers' market, and everything was quiet and serene. So, as you might imagine, it was very hard to let go—especially because the move put me in the position of breaking up with my boyfriend and bouncing from house to house working as an overnight pet-sitter. And as challenging as this has been, it has taught me so much about being present and grateful moment by moment. Money, food, clothes, friendships—resources keep appearing even though I myself have very little. That's why I think that there's something magical about this question: "What Makes You Grateful?" It rolls around in your head until your heart opens, your eyes soften, and your whole life begins to reorganize.

At least that's what's happening for me.

So if you're having trouble seeing the good, it's OK. Gratitude is hard work. It is not easy to be grateful sometimes, especially when you're in the middle of a loss or transition. *Yet it's possible.* So wherever you are, whatever you're doing, take a moment to contemplate: What makes YOU grateful? You don't have to know it now. Just ask the question. Sit with it. And let yourself be inspired by the many voices within this book.

> *Listen to the beating of your own heart. It is speaking to you now,*
> *waiting for you to hear it and respond to its call of love.*
> —*Anne Kubitsky*

Participant Donna Marie Joyce, Esq., writes:

I am so captivated by the project, which [has] stirred a powerful energy and evolution in our collective conscience—awakening the grateful heart. As someone who studied international law and politics, I cannot help but think on a daily basis now what something as elemental as a grateful heart could mean for world peace, particularly should more and more people look at life through this lens . . . This is why I am so joyous and, indeed, humbled to be part of this project. I am thankful for the space [this] created in my life, and in this world, by encouraging an attitude of gratefulness . . .

A. Shpitalnik, Russia

Love people love people love people love A. Shpitalnik Russia

Ich bin dankbar für meine große Familie, meine gute Freunde und alle Leute, die ich kenne.

"I'm grateful for my big family, good friends and all people I know"

—Anna Shpitalnik

* To see this postcard, please go to page 149.

PMC 14NOV11 ML

WHAT I'M GRATEFUL FOR
P. O. BOX 602
OLD LYME, CT 06371

"Listen to the silent exchange of and you will be forever grateful"
14/11/2011 - MO

I met this Cambodian family as offered me a ride across the Tonle S the middle of the night, having gotte on a far shore. As a photojournalist seen many hardships in people's lives, yet meeting left me with a new friendship I took the family to my heart as my own providing health care and other necessit through the help of friends in There comes a point cannot perceive

Some Look for the Good Project installations and events . . .

What a gorgeous day!! Birds are ensconced in performing a perky sunrise overture to welcome this morning. Orange blossoms are sharing their essence of delight through their sweet fragrance. Beautiful daughters still dreaming peacefully. Into the garden with Bilbo (our handsome Jack Russell) I go . . .

Life is delicious!

—Jennifer

What I'm Grateful For

PO BOX 602

OLD LYME, CT 06371

USA

FIRST CLASS

Close your eyes and take a deep breath. You are ALIVE! Life is the most precious gift. Yet how often do we take the time to notice it? The fact that a trillion cells are working right now to ensure that you are conscious and able to read this book is a miracle! To be awake . . . alive . . . to feel . . . to see . . . to taste . . . to hear . . . everything is a gift. And to receive these gifts, all we need is gratitude.

—AOK

"Congratulations! You're alive! If that's not something to smile about, I don't know what is."

—Anonymous

Joe Galiette writes:

Since I was three years old, I spent two weeks every September in an oxygen tent recovering from a yearly bout with asthma. When I was six, I took voice lessons to help me control my breath. But it wasn't until I was twelve that I finally got the asthma under control. The early signs and symptoms alerted me to do some relaxation and breathing exercises and I would stop whatever I was doing to take care of myself.

I think this is why I excelled so much at sports. With pure oxygen nourishing my cells for two weeks every year as a child, I seemed to have sharper senses than my peers. I could see farther, hear better, and jump higher than my friends. To me, I just thought the others were lazy, and it wasn't until high school that I realized I had some gifts. I excelled in baseball, football, track, tennis, and was offered a full scholarship to three colleges, including Notre Dame for football, and the University of Hartford for tennis. I didn't take them because I was already married and settled into a blue-collar life that I thought was going to make me very happy and successful.

However, eleven months into my marriage, I was drafted into the army and spent my first anniversary in basic training. I trained as an infantryman for deployment to Vietnam. When I was inducted, I told them I had a history of asthma and the recruiting officer said it didn't apply to me since I hadn't been treated for it for almost ten years. That realized, I conceded to my sense of ethics and tried my best to be a good soldier. Although my asthma often got in the way, I did my best to be all I could be and quickly advanced to the "Point" position in my platoon. The Point is the scout soldier, usually thirty meters ahead of everyone else. And as I trained for this, I became more and more prone to asthma attacks.

By the time we were scheduled to deploy in two days, I was coughing with every breath—hardly the condition I should be in to do my job. We were quarantined and confined to our barracks, rendering it against military orders to move around the

compound. By threat of court martial, anyone violating this order would be tried for desertion. But I couldn't be deployed with this condition. I needed medicine to quiet the cough. My platoon was relying on me. Although my Superior Officers forbade it, I made my way to the hospital to see the doctor. My regular doctor wasn't there and instead, there was a Sergeant Major filling in. I told my story and he listened attentively. When he heard enough, he stopped me and asked if I could wait in his office. In a few minutes he joined me with a huge book in his hands. I commented on its size and wondered if he would possibly find the right medicine in it. He flipped page after page until he exclaimed, "Here's what I'm looking for!" He looked at me and said, "Son, you're going home. The army regulation I'll read you specifically directs that no one with a history of asthma shall be allowed into the military." He prescribed some medicine and ordered a battery of tests to determine my sensitivities. He wrote an order to my captain to release me immediately.

It took two more months to process me off the base. During that time, half my unit was killed in the first deployment. Even if I had been there, I was told by wounded returnees that there would have been nothing I could have done—the choppers dropped the platoon right into an ambush. At the time, my wife was eight months pregnant.

I am grateful for the affliction that kept me on the sidelines and saved my life; I am grateful to have been there when my Trisha and Jason were born. All that came after is the proverbial and grateful icing on the cake.

What are you grateful for in *your* life?

What does gratitude mean to you? Why does life itself make you grateful?

I am grateful to be ALIVE! It is so awesome. Possibilities are limitless and there's so much to learn, do, make, experience! Holy wow! I am surrounded by AWESOME! It ripples around me. Womp womp womp womp.

—Ashley Newton

TOAD—day is a good day!

—Sara Drought Nebel

I am grateful for...
EACH DAY

—Maureen Kennedy

I am grateful for…

art poet
HEALTH
peace s
WISDOM
spirituali
FAMILY   LOVE
harmor
generosi
SIMPLICITY

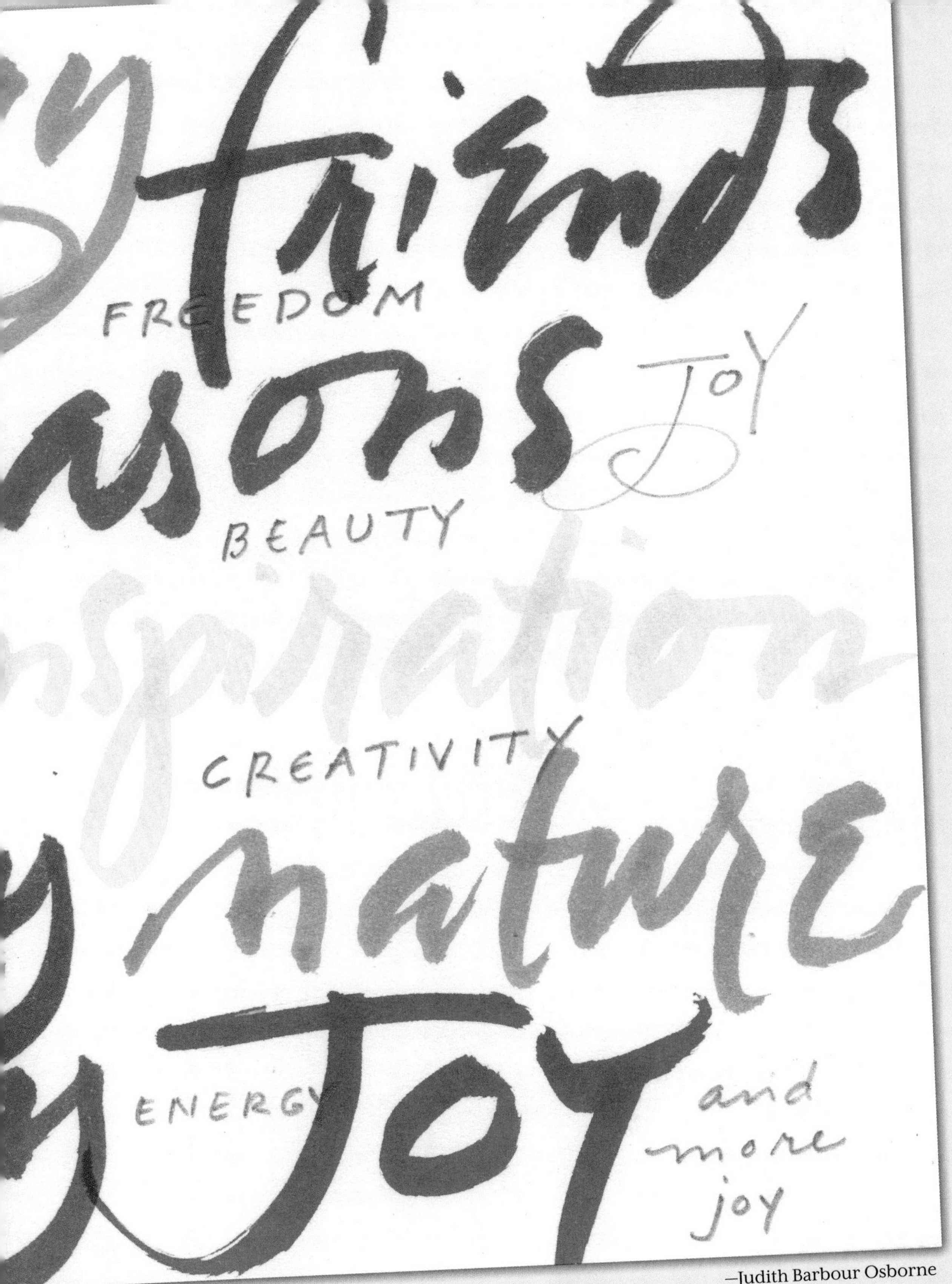

friends

FREEDOM

reasons JOY

BEAUTY

inspiration

CREATIVITY

nature

ENERGY JOY and more joy

—Judith Barbour Osborne

Hello. I'm 72 years old. This is my first watercolor painting. I had never been able to attend art school, had never explored the world of art. In 2009 I met a woman who had been wrongfully incarcerated for five years. She was a self-taught artist; a delightfully positive person, amazingly so. In 2011, just a year ago, she asked me if I would be interested in joining a class she was taking with nationally acclaimed watercolorist, Beth Patterson. I was accepted, and the experience of painting—of painting in watercolor—has changed my life. I will always be grateful to my friend "K."

—Gail Barringer

I am grateful for my mother's hands which sewed my clothes when I was young (even though I wanted "store bought" fashions). She informed my hands so that mine could sew my daughter's prom gown because she wanted something "more special than store bought." In my daughter's hands is my mother's inspiration, for she has inherited her love of quilting as shown by the quilt she made for her [own] daughter.

 I wonder if my granddaughter will sew?

—Laurel Friedmann

I am grateful for the freedom of speech, and for brave young women who keep it real.

—From "Occupy Wall Street" in 2011, before it was disbanded

I am grateful for the sun, the moon, and the stars; the love that envelops me, and that I can give back to this lovely world.

—Janet Lee

I'm grateful that I'm 91 years old and still painting! I'm grateful for lovely Maggie Valley in Haywood County, North Carolina.
—Denise Mccullough

I am very grateful for being alive. Sixteen months ago I could not sleep and the next day I decided it was time to divorce after a 25 years marriage. Today I am so grateful I had the strenght to get out of a not healthy relationship. Today I Have a voice !!!

—Anonymous

What I'm Greatful for in the and we will conserve only what we love. We will love only what we understand. We will understand only what we are taught.

I am greatful for that the animals is our sweet friends.

Form strategic partnerships.

I am greatful for the fact that nature always amazes us...

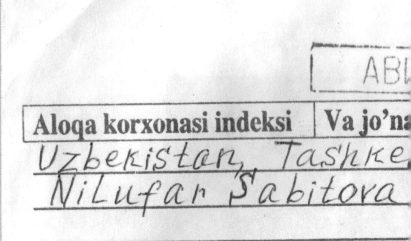

Aloqa korxonasi indeksi	Va jo'na...

Uzbekistan, Tashke...
Nilufar Sabitova

ABK

O'ZBEKISTON POCHTASI

0637180

I am greateful for that the world is colorful and beautiful.

TOP LEFT: ". . . in the end, we will conserve only what we love. We will love only what we under-stand. We will understand only what we are taught." MIDDLE LEFT: "I am grateful for that the ani-mals is our sweet friends." BOTTOM LEFT: "I am grateful for the fact that nature always amazes us."
ABOVE: "I am greateful for that the world is colorful and beautiful."

—Nilufar Sabitova

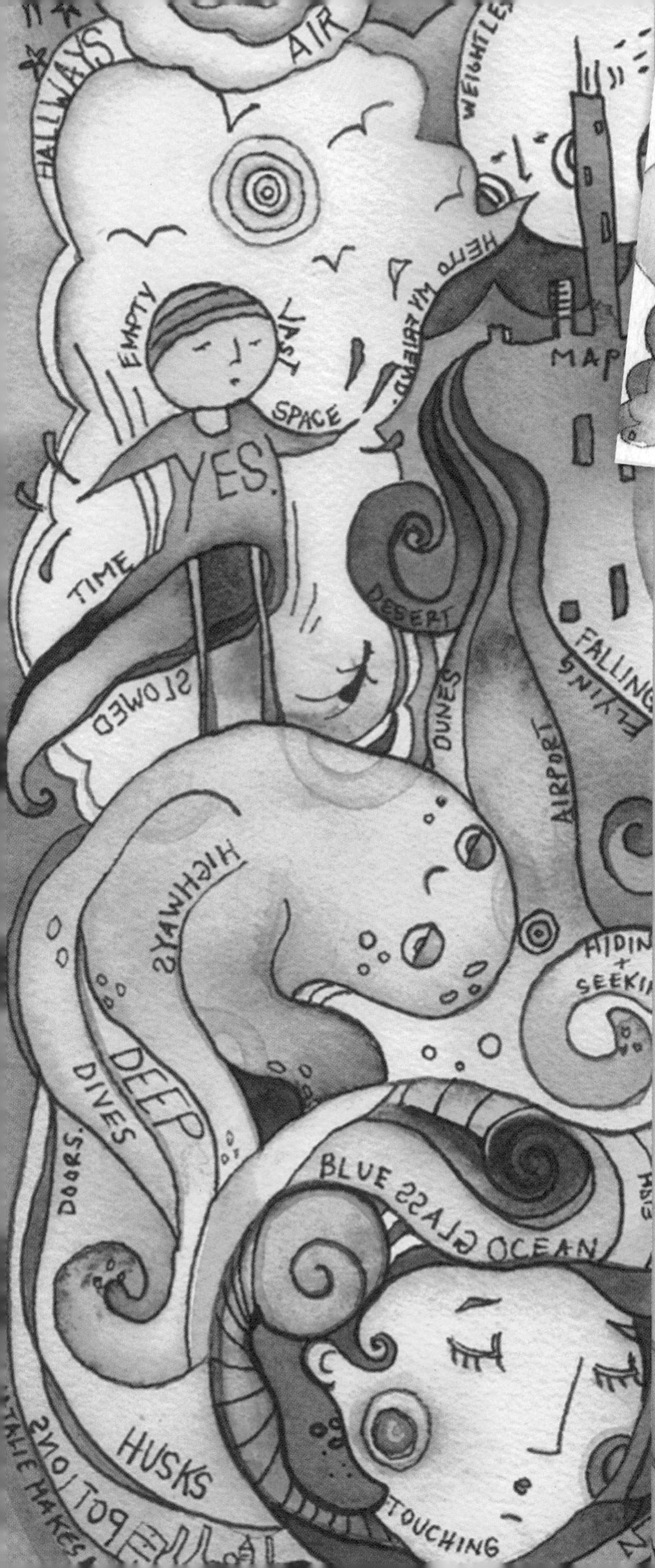

I AM GRATEFUL FOR VIVID DREAMS

—NATALIE, PORTLAND CT

I am grateful for the connectedness of my being. Waves of energy, bursts of electricity, and the spaces between that allow for endless possibilities. I am grateful for vivid dreams.

—Natalie Banker

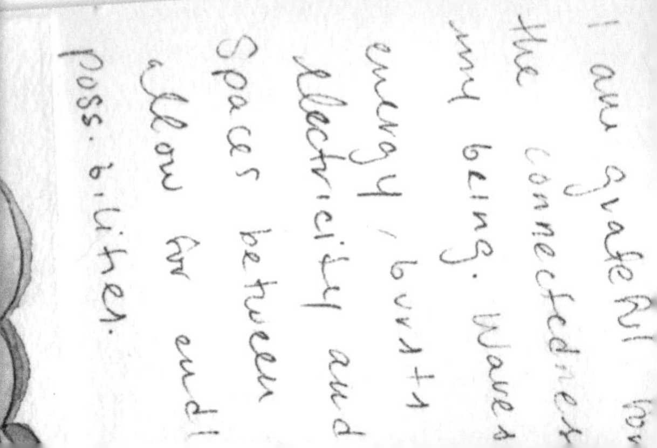

I am grateful
For the Meditative
Place that whittling
Takes Me.

—Noah Kaeser

Noah Kaeser

What I'm Grateful For
PO Box 602
Old Lyme, CT 06371

Noah is a violin maker. This postcard is a self-portrait of his hands carving the scroll-end of a violin in his signature style.

I am grateful
for things
that make me
smile :)

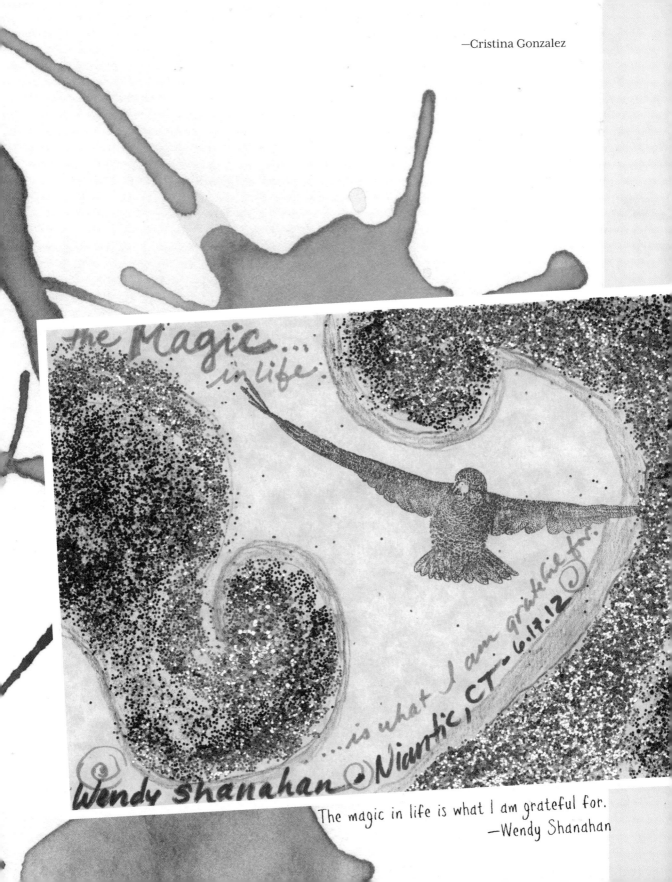

the Magic... in life

Wendy Shanahan ● Niantic, CT ● 6.17.12

...is what I am grateful for.

The magic in life is what I am grateful for.
—Wendy Shanahan

I'm grateful for **love**

Love is our life force, our breath, our one true context. And as long as you are alive, there will never be a time when you will run out of love. But love takes courage. In order to taste its sweet nectar, you must also be willing to face the bitterness of pain. When we surrender to love and allow it to lead, kindness awakens. Life is love, and you are part of it.

—AOK

"You yourself, as much as anybody in the entire universe, deserve your love and affection."

—Buddha

Birth Doula Amy May writes:

Dear Mama,

I spent Thursday night next to you, the last full night before you died. You slept fitfully in the reclining chair, and I rested on the couch with my baby daughter asleep on my chest. You hardly slept and woke often to tell me something important or to ask for help, even though it took great effort to talk.

Once you told me enthusiastically, "Honey sticks are *great!*" The honey tasted good to you and eased the discomfort of your sore mouth. Another time you woke with, "Palesa is so precious, she is just so precious." I'm so thankful you got to meet Palesa and spend time together. She was born soon after you were diagnosed, and she was almost ten months when you died. I'll never forget you playing "Let's Bonk Heads" with her, or singing, "Zoom, Zoom, Zoom, We're Going to the Moon." I'll also remember how you sternly reminded me that it was *your* song to sing to her when you caught me singing it.

You and Palesa also shared a special bond. Since Palesa was just weeks old, I started pumping precious ounces of breast milk to share with you. You called it "fortified milk" and made smoothies with it daily. We were convinced the antibodies would keep your immune system strong during six rounds of toxic chemo treatment. It did—you stayed healthy during both chemo and radiation. We were confident this secret weapon would help cure you despite the dim odds at your initial diagnosis of stage three triple-negative breast cancer. It turns out the cancer was too aggressive, deadly, and resistant to drug treatment. Still, you and Palesa shared a special connection because you were both nourished by the same milk. You breastfed me as a baby, and I am thankful I had a chance to nourish you in return.

The last night before you died, you woke me to get you a pen and paper, because you had something important to write. I never got them, instead telling you it was time to go to sleep and gain your strength to begin chemotherapy the next morning. Later, the oncologist told you that you were too weak for chemo, and you died that same night, at home in your chair. What would you have written? You insisted that it was very, very important. What did you have to say?

You called out to me again and woke me to get you ice cream—Häagen Dazs Dulce de Leche. We all hoped ice cream would help fatten you up. I grumbled about being awake, still exhausted after assisting at a birth earlier in the week. You apologized for being a burden. As tired as I was, I told you no, it is my pleasure and honor to get you ice cream and to serve my mother. I told you how much I loved you and how proud I was to be your daughter. Minutes later, as you caught your breath and found the strength to speak, you also told me how much you loved us, and how proud you were to be our mother. I believe you knew you had very little time left, though you hid it well, and it was this moment you chose to say goodbye.

When I kissed you goodbye Friday morning, I had no idea it would be our last time to see each other. I think about all the things I would have told you. I would have stayed up talking with you all night. I thought we had months left, maybe a year even. You were adamant about not being sick, and you hid it well, even when the cancer returned. You never complained, though you must have been in pain after the cancer spread to your bones. I wish I had known that the end was close. We all were caught off guard, though looking back, it was obvious that you were in the midst of dying.

The night you died, a home nurse came over for a few hours. She later reached out to us, profoundly impacted by what she witnessed. She shared in great detail about her brief time with you. Your dying experience was as close to a birth as anything she had witnessed. I was with your mother, my grandma, when she passed, and together with my aunt, we assisted as midwives in her dying process. At that point I became very aware that birth and death were not very far apart—just two different doors on opposite sides of life.

When I gave birth to Palesa, you were supportive of our decision to birth her at home. And, in the same way we chose to be "homebirthers," you were intentional about being a "homedyer." You died at home without drugs, pain medication, interruptions, or beeping machines. The nurse described you working very hard but remaining focused and present. Once, you asked for a big glass of milk—claiming you needed the milk to make you strong, because you had drunk milk when you were in labor. The nurse noticed that your process seemed a lot like labor, especially the way you instinctually moved and moaned softly. You agreed, it WAS like labor. I know giving birth was unknown and hard, but I also know that you both labored and died peacefully and without fear. You were brave, strong, and trusted the process.

It still doesn't seem real that you died. I think about you often. One of the hardest parts is the realization that I can't pick up the phone and call. But you visit me often in dreams, and I'm thankful to spend that time with you and to see you healthy and whole. I wonder often about the bond you shared with my daughter, because I still see this connection in her. When I look at her, I think of you and am thankful to remember you through her. I still play "Let's Bonk Heads" with her and sing, "Zoom, Zoom, Zoom, We're Going to the Moon," all the time. Even though it's *your* song with Palesa, I'm so thankful that I can share it with her still. You planned to live to be 100 years old, so I feel sad about the 37 years we didn't get. But for the 30 years I had with you, you were the best mom I could ever imagine. I am so thankful to have you as my mother. Now that I am a mother myself, I understand just how fiercely you loved my sister and myself, and I love you just the same.

Love,
Amy

Amy's daughter, Palesa

Amy with her mother, Nancy Louise Benson
(August 23, 1948–August 11, 2012)

Photo by Amy's sister, Karen Horn

may i open my eyes to love

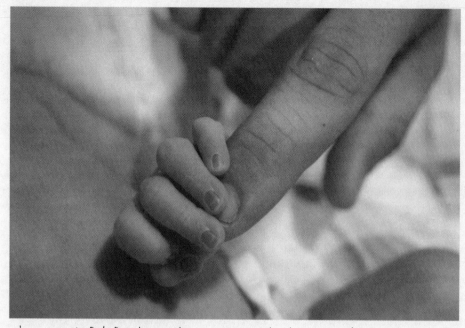

I am grateful for hope that comes with the arrival of a new baby. I am grateful for my grandchildren who remind me of small gifts in this world: the clouds, rocks, worms; the importance of laughter. The warmth of another's hand.

—Betsy Devany

I'm soo . . . grateful for whoever is reading this. U R pretty.
—Abby (age 12)
Written in lipstick on a mirror

How are you finding love in *your* life?

What does love mean to you? Why does love make you grateful?

I am finding but through
life and friends and family.
Love means happyness.
Love makes me grateful
because I know whoever loves
me is grateful for me and will
always love me from disney land
and back 1,0000,600,000,000
Times.

Bella

I know it's not a postcard, yet it's still a small message that I not only send to you, but to the whole world. It's to dare to love. This is a picture of myself and my mother, walking in the forest on a sunny day . . . The person I love the most does not exist in my world. Love is within me. I know that for I can give it, and keep giving it. But I don't take it for granted. I am very grateful to be who I am, and a very large part of that I have received from my mother. She has shown me more about love and freedom than anyone I know, just by being the most unselfish, humble, and loving being I know. I am grateful Fayza is my mother. I am grateful she is alive. And I am grateful for what I have received from her. For I wouldn't be "I" without it.

—Mohammed Massoud Morsi

ANNE KUBITSKY
LOOK FOR THE GOOD PROJECT
P.O. BOX 602
OLD LYME
CT. 06371

32

Border text (clockwise from top):

— myself — my husband — my kids — my dog — my health — my spirit — my friends — my work — my dreams — all events & people in my life, 'good' & 'bad' — The natural world & all it's magic — The endless chances to create —

I AM GRATEFUL FOR:

I am grateful to be ALIVE every day — and I'm grateful that I learned to be grateful.

It's a wonderful world...

33

Give your ♥ your 2 LOVE & Life

—Phyllis Jaffe

—Sarah Olson

I am grateful to
my JaKey 
who always
made me smile
and brought out the
most Love and compassion
in me ~

I am
grateful
to my
WIfe
who
Keeps
me anchored
and loves the Ocean

I am grateful to my pets and
All my clients who Help me
grow and LOVE   Family Top! :)

I AM MOST for
GRATEFUL LOVE

Doug Gomez 3/22/12

—Doug Gomez

I'm grateful for my life &
for my husband's life & for the
fact that we met even though
we were born 10,000 miles
apart.

—Anonymous

Painting by Diana Lyn Cote

I am grateful for kites in the breeze, for marshes and meadows, forests and trees, for waves on the beach and seals on the rocks, for friendly smiles from strangers, for the courage to smile back, and I'm grateful for gratitude which has brought me back to the center: LOVE.

—Caryl Anderson

I'm grateful for having had the experience of being deeply in love. Even though the relationship ultimately ended, it's something I'll never forget.

Because I'm
not here...

Image sent by Kate Baron. Her husband had
left this for her when he was traveling.

{There is something that you can do better than any other}

To BE able to spend time with my three original, creative, beautiful childr every day... To be able to read to them, listen to them sing, watch them dance, to tuck them into bed every night, to feel their warm arm's giving me hugs, and to share them with my husban and best friend, for this I am forever GRATEFUL

B. RUCCI

with love,
THE RUCCI
FAMILY

Everyone is a "me" or an "I."
Everyone who is born, will live,
and someday, die.
In that flicker of time in between,
everything through his eyes, is seen
like no one else who came before,
or who will, forever more.
The essence of a soul can rise,
to be seen only by another's eyes,
and when those eyes meet
—face to face—
a "spirit bridge" in earthly space,
connects them with invisible force
where Compassion can begin its course.

—Sara Drought Nebel

I'm grateful for **beauty**

Open your eyes and look around! Beauty is EVERY-
WHERE. It is in a blade of grass . . . the dewdrops of
morning . . . the tenderness between mother and child.
When we dig deep, beauty emerges. Take the time to
appreciate the beauty in all things. Life is beauty . . .
and you are beautiful.

—AOK

"For beautiful eyes, look for the good in others; for
beautiful lips, speak only words of kindness; and
for poise, walk with the knowledge that you are
never alone."

—Audrey Hepburn

Lon Cameron, repurposer of abandoned familiars, writes:

Part of what I find so ceaselessly fascinating with beauty is the fact that it really is everywhere. From the roadside freebies to the scavenged utensil—they each instigate a challenge for me to redefine with a new, functional purpose. That's why I think beauty comes from the potential that any one thing possesses, and my creative ability to harness that potential and let it shine forth.

Through the use of library books and online videos (and a particularly meager salary), I managed to construct a beautifully simple 200-square-foot house that I am all too happy to call my home. I am grateful for its bowling alley countertop, for its salvaged metal kitchen cabinetry, and for the reclaimed doors and windows left over from others' rehabilitation projects. I am also grateful for the simplistic living that my home provides. The lack of stress and clutter alone serves as evidence to one of the more satisfying manifestations of beauty: peace.

Photo by Sarah Bostick

Photo by Lon Cameron

While it is often difficult to look beyond the negatives associated with everyday life, I am constantly inspired by the ability to reframe and redirect negative energy into something more productive, more fulfilling, and . . . well . . . beautiful. Sometimes it's just fun to take a look around. Life's not about what I don't have or what I wish I had, it's about the enjoyment—and challenge—in learning to embrace the beauty of everything that surrounds me. I believe a happy life arises when we take the time to appreciate simple pleasures. And as far as having the opportunity to pursue this, I am exceedingly grateful.

Lon and his bowling alley countertop

Photos by Nicole Manganelli and Lon Cameron

How are you finding beauty in *your* life?

What does beauty mean to you? Why does beauty make you grateful?

Inspiration can spill over onto you in a moment, and suddenly you somehow find yourself swimming in a limitless ocean. It was like this for me after having been invited to a Thankfulness Brunch in December 2011. The purpose was to describe on a postcard what we each might be thankful for. I painted a sunrise. Okay, two. That was what I left there. What I took away was a wakeful and refreshed outlook . . . I couldn't stop making these little postcard paintings . . . so what I've decided to do is commit to a year's worth of creating one each day.

—Diana Lyn Cote

Diana painted 366 grateful moments in 2012 (it was a leap year)—one per day.

Her first postcard:

"This moment."

Where to begin? I am grateful for life. I am blessed to be born into the family I have. I am grateful for unconditional love, beauty, passion. I am grateful for experiences good & bad, learning & feeling. I am thankful to be 38 and to have a grasp on what's important and what's not. I am grateful for magical moments and sunny days. I am thankful for rainy days too! I am thankful for the breeze against my cheek and the breath of my babies. But most of all — I am thankful for my family — without them, none of the above would matter because I wouldn't understand it the way I do now; my grandparents, mother, father, sister, husband & children have given me so much love and strength, unconditional, love & support, joy, knowledge, tenderness. and I am blessed to walk hand in hand with each & every one of them — to hear their thoughts, share their values and learn of their passions. I am honored to be a part of them & their lives. Thank you for sharing your heart & soul with me. Thank you for your honesty, loyalty & love. Thank you for your laughter & your crying and for knowing you can always count on me just as I know I can trust in you. Nicole

After a yearlong journey painting 366 grateful moments, Diana Lyn Cote writes:

When I began this postcard-a-day project, the scope of the actual yearlong commitment was unknowable. Now, having experienced what the commitment truly means, it occurs to me to say simply but powerfully this: Initially, I thought I chose to do it. Instead, quite clearly, it has chosen me. And for that I feel a sense of honor, to represent something calling to be explored each day, that others have come along on the adventure, and that in the end it will leave me more inspired as it journeys on its forever unknowable way.

Images by Diana Lyn Cote

The fawn who visits outside of my art studio fills me with gratitude that she feels safe enough to come close and linger. I am grateful for her and my woodsy art sanctuary, and for my husband and children who believe in me and my creative pursuits . . . I am grateful for diversity and mystery of humans and the hope of unity and harmony; for a helping hand and a bowl of chicken soup for me and those who are hungry; for recoveries and awakenings; for bird symphonies at dawn and the aroma of freshly brewed coffee; [I am] grateful for water, air, rain, and sunshine; hydrangeas and sunflowers and organic food; the smooth rhythm of jazz and the soft voice of Maya Angelou; for Art that sings with color and expression, innovation, and honesty with messages, madness, or marvel. I'm thankful for hugs, smiles, and the capacity to love and be loved, to touch and explore the senses, embracing the world all around; for respect of the most common as well as the most extraordinary, and the freedom to think, learn, speak, and decide; the taste of hot buttered rolls and homemade ice cream; the students who have filled my teaching career with delight and inspiration; insight and wonder; heartfelt gratitude for memories, moments, and this opportunity to reflect and feel inspired through this sensational project . . . [which is] creating a collage of people, ponderings, pleasures, poetry, and peace.

y art studio fills me with gratitude...that she feels safe eno
grateful for her & for my woodsy art sanctuary...and for
e in me & my creative pursuits...my appreciation extends
ed the happiest childhood for me & nurtured my artistic
ple the true meaning of family, friends, love & life...the sm
& thankfulness such as a warm breeze upon my face, ripp
g paint & a card in my mailbox from a friend...I am grate
of our daughter's voice...& the image of our son on SKYP

Bright memories of their childhood evoke deep gratitude
discovery, zeal and laughter...so many fantastic wonders
rom the majestic Grand Canyon to the Ancient Puebloar
and recipes...a spider weaving her web is a site to behold
versity & mystery of humans & the hope of unity & harmor
chicken soup for me & those who are hungry...for recover
es at dawn & the aroma of freshly brewed coffee...grateful
ydrangeas & sunflowers & organic food...the smoothing
els for Art that sings with color & expression, innovation
ss or marvel...I'm thankful for hugs, smiles & the capacity
plore the senses, embracing the world all around...for resp
the most extraordinary & the freedom to think, learn, spe
d rolls & home made ice cream...students who have filled
inspiration...insight & wonder...heartfelt gratitude for mem

—Barbara Scavotto-Earley

I'm grateful for my health, for waking up every day, for seeing the sunrise and sunset, for my family, for my friends, for my job, for having money to eat, to travel, to buy the things I need. I'm very happy with my life.

Karina
(from Brazil)

I am truly grateful for beauty — in nature, in people, in form, colors, & shapes, in literature, in music, in movement, in animals — all forms of beauty. I'm grateful there is a wealth of beauty.

Mary McCarthy
Madison, Ct.

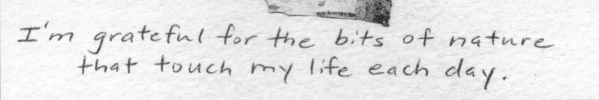

I'm grateful for the bits of nature that touch my life each day.

—Becky Brockman-Schneider

Grateful for who I am and who I am becoming. Grateful for all that inspires, uplifts, and sustains the beauty in this life. —Anonymous

I'm so super grateful for waking up every morning knowing it will be another beautiful day doing what I love most.

—Kristin

15/05/2012
GÖTEBORG, SWEDEN

SVERIGE 12 KR

PRIORITAIRE
1·a-klassbrev

To K...
h...
" I'm
up e...
one a...
I love

See yourself in others.
Change for the better when "Looking for the Good."
—Steve Klebar

I'm grateful for...

MY SON LARRY

—Coleen Proctor

Images on both pages by Diana Lyn Cote

I'm grateful for . . .

cool cotton sheets on a hot summer night stuf
fing sandwiches after Thanksgiving hugs from
my children good health excellent creme brulee
starry nights in Maine unconditional love
from our petite pets mountains and their purple
haze in Fall laughing with my husband secrets
keys Paris and art

—Patty Devoe

I'm grateful for **health**

Even if the doctor tells you that your pulse is too high, just remember . . . you HAVE a pulse. Every day you wake up and are conscious enough to appreciate the moment, there is health. Health—in its most abstract form—is pure love, gratitude, and the complete absence of dis-ease. As we give up what we want and focus on what we have, our health improves. Gratitude opens your eyes to health and healing.

—AOK

"It is health that is real wealth and not pieces of gold and silver."

—Mahatma Gandhi

Participant IZK writes:

Last weekend I faced the helplessness of staying overnight in a hospital due to an attack of appendicitis. I am so grateful for each and every one of the unsung heroes during the night shift at the hospital. They checked in on me all the time. By the early morning, yet another phlebotomist came to take my blood. She seemed very tired and, from my promptings, she shared a recent experience that traumatized her. She was a witness to the shooting of a teenager outside a supermarket nearby. She was the only one that came to his rescue and helped him stay awake until the EMTs arrived.

Being a grandmother herself, her heart was so hurt by it all because the people who were standing around were reluctant to help the boy. She couldn't help but come to his side despite the danger of more bullets. It seemed that she needed to be there to assist the child from dying on the street alone (as he did eventually pass away). I am grateful I was there to hear her story and acknowledge how she was feeling. Even though the experience upset her, I can't help but see how wonderful it was that she was moved—propelled even—to comfort the child. I may never see her again, but I will never forget her presence of Goodness.

What is incredible now is that I can share this with a community dedicated to Gratitude. I am grateful to all who have contributed to this project as it encourages me also to share. I would like to end with a quote written by a mystic, Julian of Norwich: "All shall be well, and all shall be well, and all manner of things shall be well."

Maybe this is what it means to "Look for the Good."

I am grateful for memee letting us stay at the beach house for a week. Memee and ~~the~~ my sister

— lola

How are you finding health in *your* life?

What does health mean to you? Why does health make you grateful?

ABOVE: What I am Grateful For: Being able to hear, see, feel, touch, drive, sew, cook, make pottery, quilt, write, read, sing, walk, talk, ride a bike, garden, shovel snow, watch the sun come up and go down, feel gentle morning breezes, fly a kite, make sand-castles, paint, refinish furniture, drink wine, barbeque, sit with friends over a dinner I cooked, baking, shooting my pistol, drawing water from a pump, the sound of rain on my window, the sound of my dog snoring as she sleeps, making a child laugh, warm sand under my feet, long beach walks, walks through the woods, seeing the flag flying on the wind, baseball games, embroidering, calm people, every day of life. [I'm grateful for] my eyes, being loved, a child's laughter, tears of joy, clay, sea breezes, water, trees, books, needles and thread, doves, music, spaghetti, my home, tools, my sweetheart, my car, angels, humor, life, horses, seashells, a job I love, scissors, my dog, stars, clouds, bees, color, gentle rain, soft kisses, campfires, my cat, friends, sky, tea, flowers, the sound of birds, hay, ocean waves, [and] snowflakes. —B. Mann

NEXT PAGE: [I'm grateful for] healing. The surgeon walked into the exam room and said to Marianne, "You've just won the lottery," by which he meant the tumor in her kidney was benign! Praise God! —Jim Cassidy

The surgeon walked into the

HEAV

won the lottery," by which h
kidney w

...am room and said to Marianne: "You've just...

...ING

...ean't the tumor in her... benign! Praise God!

Jim Cassidy

thanks, Ann.

I am grateful that when my emotional life and my family relationships seemed bleak and barren, I had the grace to stumble into an "adult children of alcoholics" meeting more than twenty years ago. Through those wonderful, brave, truthful members, I learned to be grateful. Being grateful has allowed me to see beyond my daily trials, forge new relationships, [and] repair damaged ones as best as possible. Feeling grateful, truly grateful, changed my life every day thereafter. I try to the best of my ability to be grateful to everyone I come in contact with, to be grateful for every new challenging situation that makes me grow. It's not always easy, but it has saved my life.

—Anonymous
Front of postcard: Atacama Desert, Chile

my emotional life and, mo

leak and barren, I had th

Adult Children of Alcoholics

years ago. Through those

mbers, I learned to be grate

me to see beyond my daily

js, repair damaged ones as

ateful, truly grateful, changed

try to the best of my ability

in contact with, to be

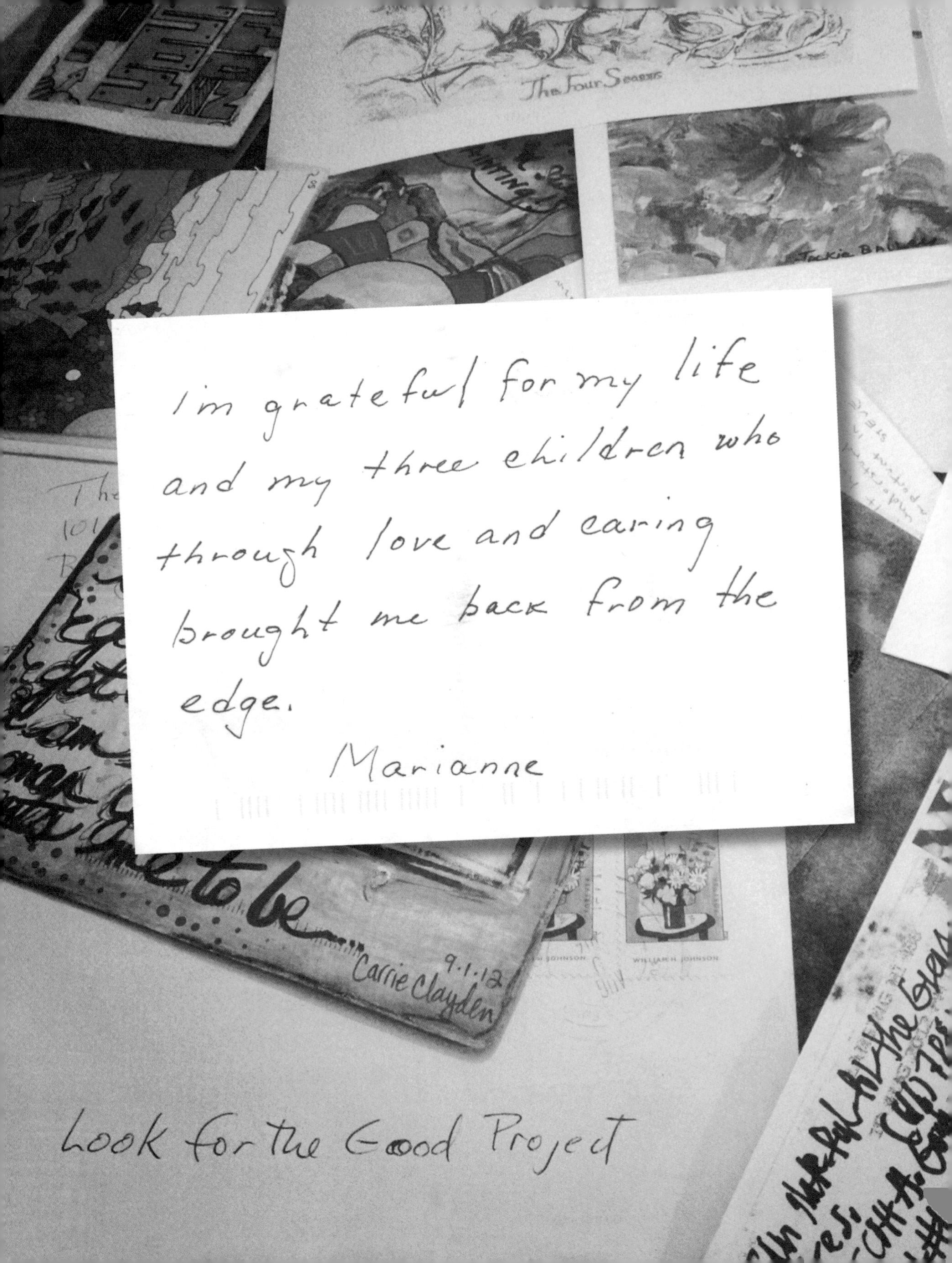

The Four Seasons
I'm grateful for my life and my three children who through love and caring brought me back from the edge.
Marianne
Carrie Clayden 9.1.12
Look for the Good Project

Image by Diana Lyn Cote

I'm grateful for the new day! I appreciate the fact that every morning we get a new sun and a new chance. You get to choose how to approach this day and what you would like to accomplish. You even get to choose nothing at all! But I have never seen anything as beautiful as a person who realizes this and chooses to make a difference. Someone who chooses *peace*. No matter what happened yesterday, there is still a choice: What are *you* going to do today?

—Jessica Johnson

I created the enclosed card: "I'm Grateful for the Honey Bee, the World's Pollinator" in memory of Brenden Stephen Foster. As you may recall from the news, Brenden Stephen Foster of Bothell, Washington, died of acute lymphoblastic leukemia in 2008 just after his eleventh birthday. But, before he died, he made national and international news for his acts of limitless kindness toward his fellow man—particularly the homeless and the underserved—and also for his concern with the earth's sustainability.

Just prior to his passing, Brenden expressed deep concern over the diminishing population of honeybees. Honeybees, as you know, are indispensable for pollination—they keep the earth's ecosystem fertile and verdant. News reports advised us that a returned pilot, in honor of Brenden, spread wildflower seeds across the world to provide nectar to the honeybees and to consequently increase honeybee populations.

In learning about Brenden's short but incredible life, all I ever could say was, "*Wow!*" Here was a child on the verge of his own death—who barely experienced life—and he was selflessly concerned with supporting and spreading life on this planet—even plant life! What a wonder worker!

Like Brenden's wildflower seeds, may this project continue to spread its positivity . . . and dwell in infinite possibility.

—Donna Marie Joyce, Esq.

All postcards by Donna Marie Joyce

This past June, I became paralyzed from the waist down after falling from high up in a tree. My recovery has been a slow process but the love and support from my community, family, and friends has been overwhelming—in a good way! I've been shown the power of love and proven to myself that even in times of crisis, there is light. Light of hope, strength, inspiration, and new opportunities that rest within the challenges. I am grateful for these gifts.

—Laurie Kammer

Laurie created the background, "Floral Emergence," as part of her art therapy.

I'm glad I got sober. I am the woman God wants me to be.
—Carrie Clayden
(Card front and back)

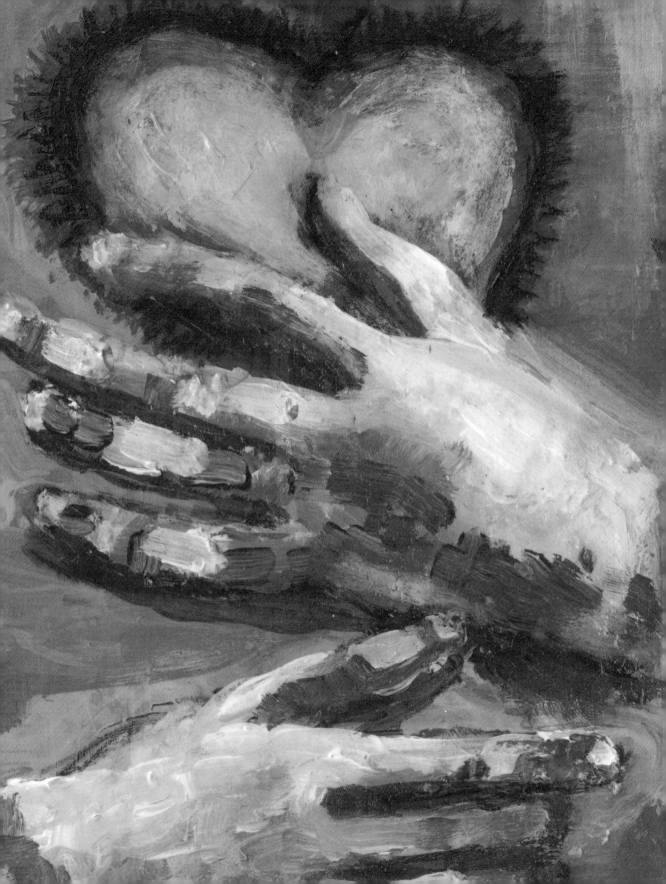

Art heals.

—Jackie Bailey

I'm Grateful for:

- <u>My Health</u>. A good friend of ours, 43 years old, was just diagnosed with stage 4 lung cancer and has tumors in his brain + in stomach. He has a 3 year old who will be a huge motivator for him so we're hoping for the best. Good health is so precious – we often overlook the value of JUST BEING HEALTHY.

—Anonymous

I'm grateful for all my yet short life experiences, and the people in them, for they have shaped the world to be a wonderful challenge

Agradezco todas las experiencias de mi aun corta vida, y las personas en ellas, ya que han hecho de mi mundo un reto maravilloso

—Anonymous

I'm grateful for my friend Andrea, who took me in, and saved my life.

Ruth

I AM Grateful WOUNDS HEAL.

—Wendy Natter

I'm grateful for **peace**

Peace is the gentle serenity that occurs when we give up what we want and allow an underlying harmony to lead. But like a rosebud, peace needs to be nurtured and given the space to bloom. If we force peace in any way, it dies. So take the time to cultivate peace. You don't have to go anywhere or do anything . . . *just let go.* The peace you're looking for is already here.

—AOK

"Peace isn't an experience free of challenges, free of rough and smooth—it's an experience that's expansive enough to include all that arises without feeling threatened."

—Pema Chödrön

Playwright Roberta Bender Silbert shares:

When my mother, at the age of 93, could no longer care for herself, she moved in with me. A brilliant and wise woman who retired at the age of 88 now had to learn to live with a brain that was slowly predeceasing her. It was as if my husband and I had adopted a disabled child.

There were the warnings against taking her in. People told me it would ruin my marriage. Even my mother, on her better days, told me I was making a big mistake.

This was the beginning of a poignant four-year journey, but the heartbreak was also heart opening. Over time I realized that this journey was a sacred one.

The fourteen journals I kept between the time she moved in with me and the time she died are a permanent record of events outside my own memory. I remember that when my father was dying, I also wrote details of every action, every glance, and every word spoken. I gave him water and broth and would count them drop by drop. I would write the date and the time and the number of drops he was able to swallow. It was as though with the right number of drops, I would be able to save him from dying of cancer. With my mother, it was as though I might find some clue to cure her dementia and—as with my father—writing my notes made me feel less helpless.

You might also want to know when I started to feel a sense of peace. It was not always so clear, but the peace began to emerge slowly. It came between the sorrow, while I was singing with her at 2 a.m. because she was afraid, while answering her bell sometimes ten times a night, after cleaning up another incident of incontinence. The peace even came after the times that I thought I could not go on but then I did.

I look back on: the 680 scarves she made for the homeless; the maybe 2,000 games of gin rummy we played; the 160 times we watched the movie *The American President*; the 5,000 times she must have rung for me, sometimes just to see if I would come and sometimes just to tell me that she loved me. Then there were all the things she could not remember, all the words she could not think of, there were all the people who just met her who knew nothing about what kind of person she was before she became ill, who knew nothing about what was inside her where there was no dementia—deep inside where she was perfect.

In the end she did not always know my name, or who I was, or who she was, or even if she was still alive. But she would still respond to my hugs. In my heart she was always my loving mother and she was always the mother I loved.

My mother did not want to go on living with dementia, and in the end she found the healing that she sought in death.

Caring for my mother gave me a tremendous sense of peace. I was this person who cared for someone with such love and kindness and compassion. This was just the kind of person I wanted to be. Along my sacred journey, my heart opened. And as my heart opened, I let the peace in—deep inside—and I became grateful for the feeling that my life was truly worthwhile.

—Anonymous

How are you finding peace in *your* life?

What does peace mean to you? Why does peace make you grateful?

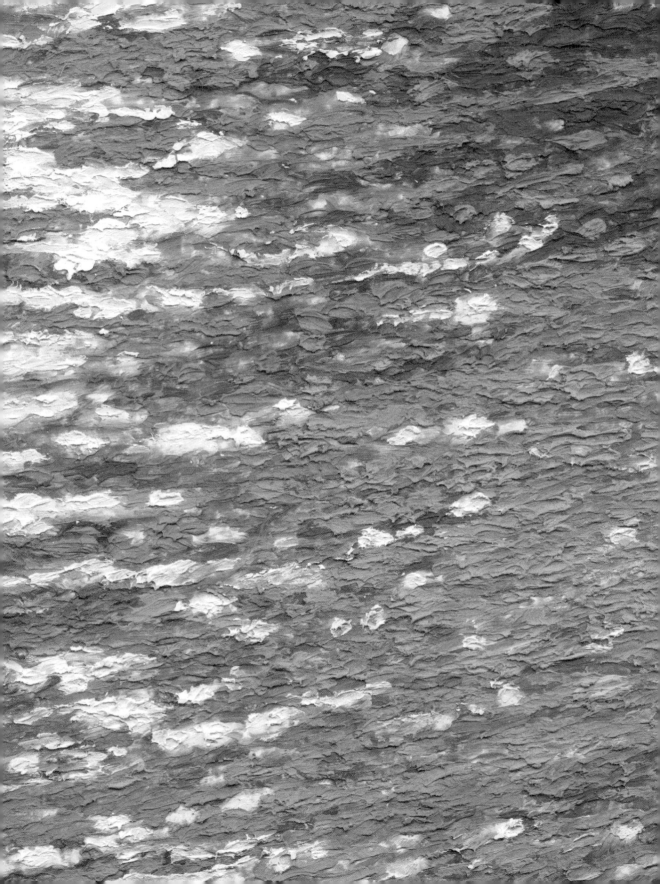

I am thankful that
I can be in this moment and
take a deep breath. When everything is swirling 'round, it is so
easy to forget. I'm thankful that
right now, I'm remembering
to B R E A T H E.

—Anonymous

Image by Diana Lyn Cote

Winter Moonrise.
—Gale Simonson

I'm grateful for silence and the ways it helps me be a better, kinder, more compassionate me!

—Anonymous

The time when I feel most grateful to be alive is on morning walks with my dad.
I'm grateful for:
my family
my Home
the sunrise
Mother Ocean
the sea critters that sustain this fishing community

—Katherine Thompson

ful I am for the indivi
activities that

eep

Steady"

Times of Si

prayer, you

on the beach

Good books + great musi

Playtime with children

tea

thanks

How grateful I am for the individuals and activities that "keep my soul steady"—spiritual guides and times of silence, yoga, meditation, prayer, journaling, long walks on the beach, meals with family and friends, good books and great music, playtime with children, conversations over tea, opportunities to give thanks—like this one!

—Anonymous

I am grateful for the air that I breathe... the water I drink... the sun that shines and warms my skin... I am grateful just to be.

—Anonymous

Momentos simples com música, comida deliciosa, e na companhia de grandes amigos.

Lisa

Simple moments with music, delicious food, and the company of great friends.

Recovery makes every borrowed day beautiful: Living in recovery from drugs and alcohol abuse makes every day and every breath a grateful one. When you are so truly broken the only thing left to do is surrender to the fact that you are powerless. From that point on you have to learn to live again. Everything in your life must change. Essentially you are reborn. I like to think of it as coming out of a basement that you have been trapped in for many years. You realize the true beauty of existence itself, things you never noticed before. The sun is warmer, the colors are brighter, even the bad days really aren't that bad. Every moment is borrowed. I know for a fact that the rest of my life will be filled with happiness. I will forever be content as long as I do the work and stay spiritually connected. For my addiction, my recovery, and my life, I am forever grateful.

—Sarah Buonocore

The pond contains awareness of both worlds,
above and below, with this gentle disturbance.
—Diana Lyn Cote

10-10-2012

I LIKE TO WALK BAREFOOT THROUGH THE FOREST AND
LOOK AT THE PLANTS AND THE ANIMALS AROUND ME
HOW THE TREES SPEAK TO ME WHEN IT'S WINDY,
I FEEL ALIVE AND HAPPY. SO GRATEFUL! WHEN I REALIZE THE
MOST IMPORTANT THINGS IN THE WORLD ARE THE SIMPLES
THINGS, SO WE DON'T HAVE TO COMPLICATE OUR LIVES, J
OBSERVE AND ENJOY THE PRESENT, BECAUSE IT IS THE O
REAL THING THAT WE HAVE NOW. / Miguel — SPAIN

Above: I like to walk barefoot through the forest and look at the plants and the animals around me . . . how the trees speak to me when it's windy, and I feel alive and happy. So grateful! When I realize that the most important things in the world are the simplest things so we don't have to complicate our lives, just observe and enjoy the present because it is the only real thing that we have now.

—Miguel

Handwritten on photo:
pportunity to know great people.

Brazil / Diego Pereira

10/10/2012

Above: I'm grateful when I meet new people, cultures and when I can teach about my values. This photo shows us that peace is possible when people respect and learn about other people . . . Now I know because I see with my own eyes that Egypt isn't the pyramids, Switzerland isn't watches, [and] Saudis aren't oil and petrol. I am lucky, because I have the opportunity to know great people.

—*Diego Pereira*

10·23·12

Dear Anne,

I'm Grateful knowing if
I have the courage to love
my life, loves, friends and
self enough to let them all
go to shine + "be" on their
own, then I will know
love and realize my potential!

leaning in,

~ Bob McCandlish

I'm grateful for the early morning
quiet softly interrupted by birdsong.
Beginning with one chirp . . . then a
few more . . . then a chorus.

—Lorre Broom

I am grateful for the beautiful colors in the sky at sunrise.

—Wendy Price

I'm grateful for **freedom**

There is something beautifully raw and unbridled—something wild, even—that comes from the heart and soul of each of us. If you try to pin it down, the purity is lost and the beauty wanes. Honor the undefined wilderness inside. Let it be. The passion of your own heart will set you free.

—AOK

FREE◗OM

"Expose yourself to your deepest fear; after that, fear has no power, and the fear of freedom shrinks and vanishes. You are free."

—Jim Morrison

Heather Scott Lagerstrom writes:

Following the very abrupt and hurtful end to a friendship, I found myself questioning why it had happened and what I had done or could do better. While the answer never truly came, the questions were, in themselves, a gift because I found myself on a path of healing, a path of self-discovery, and a path that would only make my life so much more abundant and full of blessings.

This is what I did:

I made time for myself—time to absorb the beauty that life can be, and to truly appreciate it.

I found the spiritual side of me—the side that counts her blessings every day. I took the time to listen to the wind, to look for spiritual signs, to respect Mother Nature and the elements, and to appreciate the beauty that life can share.

I found the artistic side of me—the side that found me back on stage for the first time in twenty years, all because my daughter asked me to perform alongside her. I rediscovered the passion I had for performing arts, and got to share precious and priceless moments with my daughter.

I rediscovered love—the same love that led me to marry my best friend fourteen years ago. We make time for each other. We talk about everything. We laugh. And we respect what is important in our lives and hearts. He makes me want to marry him all over.

I found pride. As I sit back and watch my daughter find her sense of self, the pride wells up inside me. Despite those crucial and tough years where the world can be cruel, she rises up above it and smiles. She is confident, smart, and strong. She is everything that I could ever hope for and so much more.

I have rediscovered true friendships—the kind that weather any storm and never fade away. The kind that span across miles and across years like there was never any time

apart. The kind of commitment that you hope others see in you, as you see in your-self, and all you project out into the world.

I found the healthy side of me—the side that finds joy in quiet moments. The side that relishes meditational music and waits with bated breath for a gentle sunrise walk. The side that knows laughter truly *is* the best medicine. The side that knows it is OK to put yourself first once in awhile. The side that knows that the dark clouds will soon pass and the sun will shine again. The side that knows that while one friend-ship ended, so many others have grown and been cultivated and reconnected . . . thereby showing me that life has come full circle.

All those sides are grateful that a painful end to a long-treasured friendship started this journey—the journey to healing, happiness, freedom, artistic endeavors, friend-ships, health, and the three "Ls" that guide my life: Love, Light, and Laughter. I am truly blessed and grateful to have discovered all of the elements that have shaped me and transformed my life. And lastly, I am grateful to this project for providing the vessel to convey the gratitude and share the positivity with others.

I am thankful for sunlight.
I am thankful for difference
which reminds us we are all the same.
I am thankful for love
fighting against hate.
Most of all I am thankful for freedom.
May we use it to recognize who we truly are!

—Anonymous

How are you finding freedom in *your* life?

What does freedom mean to you? Why does freedom make you grateful?

J. Boehm - Mill Valley, CA.

I'm thankful th

I do, when I do

in a two-das, "

I'm fairly conf. &

could not have c

one generation ea

Western U.S. is icing

I am thankful that I'm living where I do, when I do. As one parent in a two-dad, mixed-race family, I'm fairly confident that my family could not have come together even one generation earlier. Living in the Western U.S. is icing on the cake!

—J. Boehm

Aren't we all a work in progress? Every day we have the opportunity to work at it and start over. For that I am grateful.

—Elizabeth Casaus

There was a time when I thought my life was tragic. Now I think it was funny. It only took 43 years!

—Anonymous

The moon rides high and the sun shines bright while eagles and ospreys swing on the wind. Eyes, ears, and discernment are truly gifts to perpetuate . . .

—Sarita Van Vlek

Your a shining Star

No matter who you are

Shining bright to see

who you can truly be

i am grateful
for time spent
dancing in the
rain with my
friends.

—Cristina Gonzalez

I am grateful to have witnessed this moment: a hummingbird, drenched from the rain, peering at the sky, as I do in moments of wonder.

—Betsy Devany

Like many participants, Betsy sent in a number of cards—even helping to distribute the invitation to others. All cards on this page are by Betsy.

When I reflect on freedom, what comes up in me is freedom from myself, the "self" that sees me as being separate from the world. I have realized freedom in the infinite universal space within myself that is love and unlimited power (creative force), and it is through this foundation that I choose seeing over neglect, ease over crisis, and love over fear. I am grateful for these gifts of freedom, as they help me take conscious responsibility for my thoughts and actions so that I may be in loving service to others.

—Lisa Sobolewski

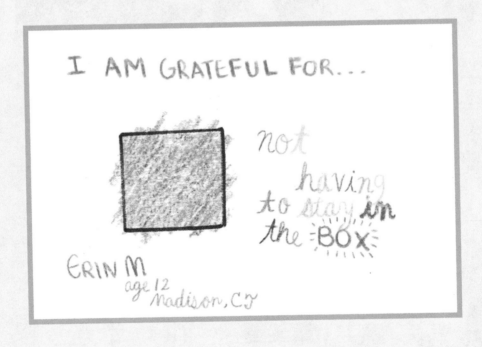

I am grateful for being able to travel freely, and to have had the opportunity to visit beautiful places around the world. I have met so many wonderful people who have enriched my life.

—Dan Yagmin Jr.

an angel i'm not

gratefully!

—Jill Butler

i am grateful for second chances!!!

—Wendy Natter

Background images by Diana Lyn Cote

People are so angry these days about not having everything the way they want it. After the Second World War in England, we had very little food, for which we stood in line for over an hour, electricity was limited, and often only candles were available, but you never heard such anger as we do today. People have had it easy for so long, they have forgotten to be grateful for what they do have.

I was sitting up during the night and was thinking for probably a few minutes before I went to sleep. I kept asking myself "What am I grateful for?"

This is probably the hardest question I have ever been asked. There are so many things that I thought of, such as medicine, doctors, humanity, hope, faith, love, and, of course, peanut butter because I love peanut butter.

After this question racked my brain for almost 24 hours, I thought about what my mother would be grateful for. So after thinking about her life in the Philippines and seeing my family there once when I was younger, I am grateful for being blessed to live in America. This country, while some people don't agree with me, gives me the freedom to pursue my dreams and hopes. I am so grateful to live in a place where so many people can come together and share their cultures from their homelands and personal beliefs freely. As a Christian I think it's important to have a strong belief, but I also value the other people around me. To be in a country that is so diverse is very beautiful and to have the freedom to have a better opportunity for income here and to send these blessings over to my family . . . [it] fills me up with so much joy that even if I was standing in the middle of a war I would feel unsinkable.

—Anonymous

In a world with so
many problems,
a good world
will awaken.
—*Sam Fritzsche*
Written in Korean

Health Waking up every

I am most grateful that, as
a woman, I live in the United
States. Many women in this world
are not free individuals because
of male domination, cultural re-
strictions, or religious oppression.
We are, for the most part, pretty
lucky to live here.
—Jeanne Draggon

gre f, as a

cu ed States.

in this world are

duals because of

ion, cultural

religious oppres-

for the most part,

live here.

Jeanne Draggon

—Lyssa Mandel

I'm grateful for **creativity**

Take some time to laugh . . . play . . . stumble . . . and fall. When you can harness the opportunity within the challenge and the perfection within the mistake, you have tapped into a creative flow that brings about inspiration, humor, and grace.

—AOK

"There is a vitality, a life force, an energy, a quickening that is translated through you into action, and because there is only one of you in all time, this expression is unique."

—Martha Graham

Art professor Vladimir Shpitalnik shares:

Ever since I was very young, I knew I wanted to be a set designer. In the Soviet Union, the worlds of theater and film offered those who were fortunate enough to work in those industries a great deal of creative freedom. You could say whatever you wanted as long as you were creative enough to disguise it from censors. So it was a difficult but also incredible time for artists, theater people, and writers. My friends and I always worked to see between the lines. In everything and anything. We wanted to read deeper and understand more—to see what the artist was really trying to say. The pressure of regulations during that time actually helped to facilitate artists' creativity. Ironically, I noticed that some artists got lost and didn't know what to say after the collapse of the Soviet Union.

So . . . what is creativity? I think it has a lot to do with how you observe the world—essentially your perspective. You're filtering everything you see and experience through your brain and heart and creating something new. Good literature is where everything begins for me. My teacher, Valery Leventhal, is probably the most amazing, creative person I ever knew. He changed my idea about how to create things because in order to study under him, I had to forget everything I knew. It was very difficult in the beginning, because I had to let go of my preconceived notions. But now, as a teacher myself, I understand the difference between teaching someone how to paint versus teaching someone how to think, see, and question. And when students finally open their eyes to creativity, it's rewarding to see how they grow. Everything you do each day can be creative. If you approach your everyday routine with creativity, you will lead a full life, a rich life.

That's why I am so grateful for my profession. I can't imagine my life without it. It's so exciting to wake up with an idea at two o'clock in the morning and work on it all night and see how it evolves. I never feel like I'm "at work." And I get to do this every day. I really can't think of anything better.

may i open my eyes to creativity

Illustration by Vladimir Shpitalnik

How are you finding creatvity in *your* life?

What does creativity mean to you? Why does creativity make you grateful?

may i open my eyes to creativity

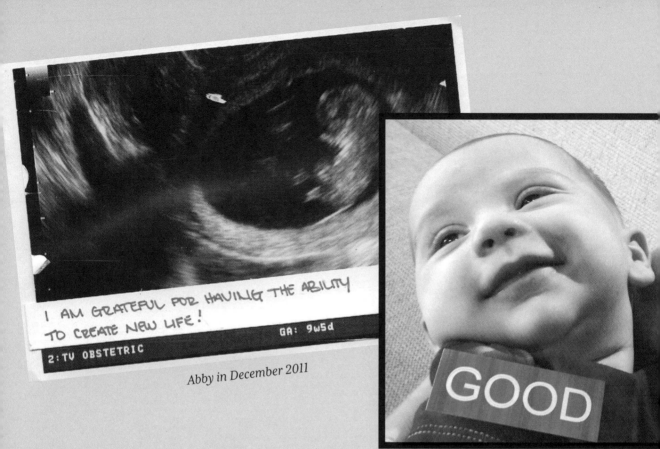

I AM GRATEFUL FOR HAVING THE ABILITY TO CREATE NEW LIFE!

2:TV OBSTETRIC   GA: 9w5d

Abby in December 2011

GOOD

Abby in the summer of 2012

GOOD

Before I found out I was pregnant, I was feeling very isolated and creatively blocked. A persistent voice was calling for change—calling for me to create something, but I had no idea where to begin. It wasn't until after I gave birth, and first set eyes on this impossibly tiny being, that I realized the persistent voice calling to me was Abby's. She has brought a beautiful vibrancy back to my life that I didn't even know was missing. I am still in shock from it all. While I was grateful for being pregnant, I was still ripping my hair out trying to figure out what I needed to *do*; I didn't realize it was already being done . . . *she* is what I needed to create.

—Erica Louise Lord Edwards

Sometimes it's more interesting to paint with the mind's eye rather than through direct observation

—Diana Lyn Cote

I am grateful for my dreams because they push me to do things that I never would have been able to do without them.

—*Van Logan Franklin*
This postcard was made out of leather.

creating
the
imagined
with
my hands

M. BOOTH
VENTURA, CA

NOV 26 PM

WHAT I'M GRATEFUL
PO BOX 602
OLD LYME CT 06371

This postcard was burned on wood.

I am grateful for the natural gifts I receive which make me create art for people to enjoy.

—Christopher Zhang
Portrait painted from
Chris' travels in Tibet

I am grateful for language that allows me to describe my passions with exquisite precision.

—Nicole Manganelli

pre·cise \pri-ˈsīs\ *adj* **1 :** exactly defined or stated : DEFINITE **2 :** highly accurate : EXACT **3 :** conforming strictly to a standard : SCRUPULOUS — **pre·cise·ly** *adv* — **pre·cise·ness** *n*

pre·ci·sion \pri-ˈsi-zhən\ *n* : the quality

I am grateful for art making—for it's aligning
me with the fundamental order of existence.

—Judith Barbour Osborne

I am grateful for all my senses so I can see colors like raspberry red, smell mudflats, hear laughter, taste chocolate (dark!), feel warm hugs, see sunrises and sunsets, smell mown grass, hear the crackle of a fire, feel sand between my toes, listen to snoring, feel cold wind on my cheeks, [and] hear giggles.

—Debbie Goodrow
This postcard was made out of clay.

Morning

Coffee

couldn't get started without it.

m—

I'm grateful for **abundance**

A gentle touch . . . a generous smile . . . a thoughtful word. Abundance is so much more than money and things. Marvel at the sheer luxury of being alive and able to experience so much! Feel the sunshine on your skin . . . listen to the rain . . . watch the people going by . . . experience the richness of *this* moment. Wherever there is a flow of appreciation and kindness, there is abundance and we somehow have everything we need—right when we need it, and not a moment before.

—AOK

What are YOU Grateful for?

"With gratitude, whatever we have is enough."

—Anonymous

Henrique Ferreira de Sousa writes:

I was born in one of the poorest neighborhoods of São Paulo. Looking back now, I can recall times when we didn't have enough to eat. It was hard for my mother to raise six kids on her own after my father tragically died of a heart attack. "Abundance" wasn't a well-used word for us back then. But in the midst of harsh conditions, my mother always made sure we had enough.

When I was seven years old, however, it became obvious to my brothers and me that my mom couldn't provide for our basic needs and, with no other choice, had to place us in an American orphanage. And, as difficult as it was, we would later find out that it was the best choice she had ever made. Not only did it help my two older brothers and me, but it has helped my entire family. Since my mother placed us in the orphanage in 1994, she has left the poor neighborhood, has gotten remarried, has a new home, and welcomed two more children into the family. Growing up at the orphanage, my brothers and I were able to overcome our past and now help various kids who are in the same conditions we started in. In fact, my brother Edinaldo and I now run the orphanage, while my older brother works in the US raising funds for us. And in addition to working, both my older brothers are attending college, which seemed an impossible dream when we were growing up.

Today I'm not rich. I don't make a lot of money. But I found out that abundance is not about money. It's about being grateful and opening your eyes to realize that you have more than enough. I can easily see abundance in my own life—abundance in what I have, abundance in joy, abundance in friendship, and abundance in love. By rekindling hope and happiness in teenagers whose parents are not capable or willing to look after them, my brothers and I have found great joy. It's rewarding to help others see the abundance in their lives—to make sure that they never have to go hungry again, to make sure that they are sheltered, and to make sure that they are loved.

I found out that when you work to give other people things in abundance, suddenly abundance becomes more apparent in your own life. Life is not about having everything you want, but simply realizing that you have everything you need. It's hard to ignore life's abundance when you look at the world with grateful eyes.

Postcards sent from Henrique's orphanage in Brazil

How are you finding abundance in *your* life?

What does abundance mean to you? Why does abundance make you grateful?

—Anonymous

bannana

macyroni

apple

greenbeens

carrits

—Philip

I'm thaikful for my family and a roof over my head

Images by Diana Lyn Cote

I am grateful for finally falling asleep last night, for getting up with the alarm, for being able to sit down for breakfast, for breakfast, for *two* walnuts in my cereal, for Thursday and yoga, for yoga teacher Barbara, for 70 years of life, for whatever good eating habits I have, for the miracle of days without pain, for the impermanence of early morning aches, for the sweetness of my grandsons, for good friends, for the wool blankets on my bed, for the teachings of the Buddha as passed on by Thich Nhat Hanh, his student Joanne Friday and his monastics, for dental floss when it does not shed or stick to my teeth, for bringing a smile to others, for walking weather and cooperative legs and feet, for tasks accomplished and tasks waiting to be done, for a working iron, my warm thrift-shop sweater, a seasonable November chill, for two consecutive nights' sleep without Ambien, for Christopher knocking at my door, for being able to help him, for a pistachio in my cereal, for a working washing machine, a new day, mechanical pencils, phone cards, sciatica in remission, swiss chard, kale, collards, Bengal Spice Tea, Crazy Burger, patient mentors, that what just leaped out of my hands and onto the floor didn't break, clerks that go the extra mile, flexibility, sunshine, avocados, for finding an outlet from which I can remove the cord of the iron without yanking, for growth that comes through difficulties, for the bottom of this card!

—Ann

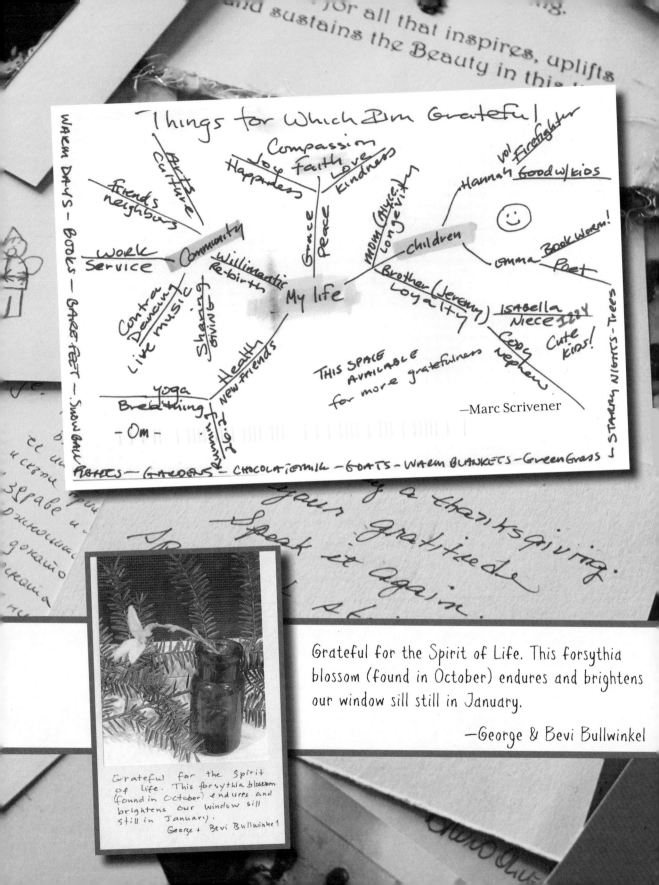

Things for Which I'm Grateful

WARM DAYS – BOOKS – BAREFEET – SnowBall – FIGHTS – GARDENS – CHOCOLATE MILK – GOATS – WARM BLANKETS – GreenGrass – Trees – STARRY NIGHTS

Better Culture
friends neighbors
WORK Service Community
Contra Dancing Live music
Sharing giving
Willimantic Re-birth
My life
Health New friends
yoga Breathing
– Om –

Compassion
Joy faith Love
Happiness Kindness
Grace Peace

vol Firefighter
Hannah Good w/ kids
children
Mom (Alyce) Longevity
Brother (Jeremy) Loyalty
Emma BOOK WORM! Poet
Isabella Niece 12/24 Cute Kids!
Cody nephew

THIS SPACE AVAILABLE for more gratefulness

—Marc Scrivener

Grateful for the Spirit of Life. This forsythia blossom (found in October) endures and brightens our window sill still in January.

—George & Bevi Bullwinkel

Grateful for the Spirit of Life. This forsythia blossom (found in October) endures and brightens our window sill still in January.
George + Bevi Bullwinkel

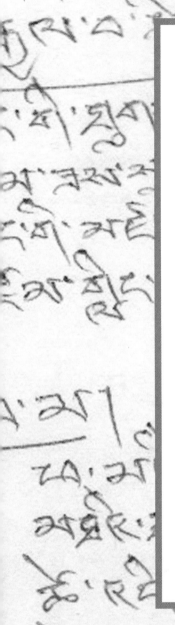

I'm Grateful . . .

For His Holiness the Dalai Lama: As a Tibetan, I'm grateful for His Holiness the Dalai Lama and the unforgettable good that he's done for the Tibetan people, "The Corn Flour Eaters," and for the world at large. His ideas and actions have had a huge impact on the world and for that I'm grateful.

For my Parents: Parents love, care, and nourish us from birth. If I tried to compare it with the immensity of the ocean, it would not be enough. That's why, if in this life, I cannot pay this back, I will keep this in my heart for the next life.

For my Brother: His love and kindness is always present with me. Right now, I am settled enough so that I can approach any circumstance, and this is because of him. I keep this always deeply in my heart and will never forget.

For America: This nation is first rank and full of educated and capable people. It appreciates all nations of this world—especially all of us Tibetans. For this we cannot forget and I say "thank you" again and again.

—*Dakpa Samdup*
Written in Tibetan

Glaciers & throat singing, friends & poems, and weather. Dialect and dialog. Wild salmon in wild rivers. Animal tracks in snow & lengthening days of spring. Coffee. Sailing. Music. Hot springs & tidepools. Thanksgiving dinner & full moons. Old typewriters that work. The Deborah Number. Diction & silence, binoculars; tides & foghorns.

for starters,
Jeremy

[I'm grateful for] Glaciers & throat singing, friends & poems, and weather. Dialect and dialog. Wild salmon in wild rivers. Animal tracks in snow & lengthening days of spring. Coffee. Sailing. Music. Hot springs & tide pools. Thanksgiving dinner & full moons. Old typewriters that work. The Deborah Number. Diction & silence, binoculars; tides & foghorns. For starters.

—Jeremy Pataky

. . . It's hard to beat nature.

—Felicia Baril

i am grateful for:

new socks

puffy jackets

hedgehogs

lakes

snow cones

swings

memories

ree
rses

lighthouses

coffee

sunglasses

crushed
ice

zen gardens

m
dry

maggie durso-smith

—Maggie Durso-Smith

Painting of Nancy & Margaret by Lisa Melmed

When my twenty-two-year-old daughter Margaret had

a brain stem stroke in May 2006, I did not ask the question, who will help me? Or, what help do I need? People stepped forward, in remarkable, often inspiring, ways. A friend created a "blog" so I could write about Margaret's condition. People figured out that I needed food. Members of my spiritual circle came to stay with Margaret at night so that I could rest. Sometimes people came simply to sit by my side. Often, words weren't necessary—a compassionate hug and a knowing glance at just the right moment meant more than words . . . Somehow, people sensed what I needed without my asking. These friends made it possible for me to survive a challenge that seemed impossible to endure.

In January 2007, I decided that Margaret should be able to travel to places that she loved. For that dream to come true, I needed to raise funds to purchase a van to transport my daughter; I set a goal of raising $35,000, which, at the time, seemed beyond reach. Finally I was ready to ask for help—and help is what I received, in great abundance. Friends were willing to run several fundraising events. Artists contributed work to silent auctions. Musicians and singers donated their performances. The local newspaper ran a story about Margaret and the help she needed. The list of contributors grew . . . and grew . . . and grew. Within six months, over 500 people had helped us reach our fundraising goal. Because of these people—these truly extraordinary people—once again Margaret can be in the world she loves.

And so I believe in community. I believe that if you ask for what you need, people will give it. And sometimes, even when you do not ask, people see what you need and come forward.

—Nancy Smith Worthen

I'm grateful for being held.
—Vanessa

141

Even in the woods, the light will somehow find its way to me.
—Diana Lyn Cote

THANK YOU
MOTHER!!
—Anonymous

I'm grateful for **insight**

Quietly we walk and gently we speak, because insight takes deep listening. So soft is its whisper that we often mistake the static in our minds for this deeper voice. Yet if we take a moment to be still, wisdom emerges. Step into the empty space of your own mind. Beneath thoughts and in between words, insight dawns.

—AOK

"We cannot solve our problems with the same level of thinking that created them."

—Albert Einstein

Massage therapist Lisa Steinberg shares:

I was born with it—the insight, the intuition, and the knowingness. For a child to know and grow this precious inner gift, there needs to be a healthy awareness that what is felt within aligns with what is being reflected to you from the adults around you. This becomes your inner voice—your greatest ally in charting the course of life. Without it, you are like a ship without a compass or a map.

And as a child, I lost it once for a very long time and in losing it, I lost myself.

You see, I was raised in a family that was deeply affected by mental illness. One parent was suffering from this illness, and the other parent tried to hide it by making things appear normal. This resulted in total confusion for my developing mind and soul. My childlike intuition was so confused by the conflict between what I felt and what I was being told, that I had to leave my body and psyche and dissociate from my experiences. The result was years of numbness, depression, anxiety, and disconnection.

Throughout my adult life, however, I was driven to find my lost self. Through the help of many wonderful people, therapies, and techniques, I reconnected with my inner knowing. And, over the years, my intuition has come back in full force.

How do I recognize intuition versus the voice of the ego? It is a voice that is kind, loving, and a guiding force—sometimes expressed in visual pictures and colors. I now know this inner voice well and have been blessed to utilize it in my own healing practice for the last twenty-plus years. It is something I rely on a daily basis.

When I first reconnected with my intuition, however, I felt that I was making it all up. But aligning with the slogan, "fake it till you make it," I went along with the insights, images, and messages . . . not quite sure about it all. Many years later, I no longer question how or why the insights come. It is a trust, a faith, but more importantly an inner listening.

For example, I am a massage therapist and last year I had a guest client come in for a massage at a spa where I work. The client told me that she had recently developed a blood clot in her leg. The conversation only took a couple minutes, but less than a month later, I developed the same symptoms—a throbbing pain in my right calf. From that short conversation a month earlier, I just "knew" it was a blood clot and went to a local emergency room right away.

After a six-hour wait, the doctor wanted to send me home with a prescription for inflammation. But again, I "knew" it was not inflammation and insisted on a blood test. The blood test showed elevation of coagulation factors. But still, he wanted to send me home. As I was signing the dismissal papers, my sister called. Since she happens to work in the medical field, she asked if they checked my lungs (they had not), so I requested this and the CAT scan showed multiple pulmonary embolisms. Long story short, I was admitted to the hospital immediately and my life was saved.

The same intuition that I thought I had lost in childhood is the same "voice" that has led me home—back to my Soul. There are no words to express the deep gratitude that I have for listening to this gentle, inner voice—including my own tenacity to never give up. I am grateful that I have found my compass; I have found my map; I have found Me.

How are you finding insight in *your* life?

What does insight mean to you? Why does insight make you grateful?

Matterhorn
4478 m / 14776

Besides many other things I am thankful for, I am thankful for the mountains. In the mountains I realize how small and weak I am, how negligible and pointless my problems are, no matter how serious they may be. Mountains give one a new perspective. In comparison to their longevity, a human life is so short. That's why every minute of it should be enjoyed to the max!

—Maria Tomasova
Written in Slovak

"Listen to the silent exchange of heartbeats and you will be forever grateful"
14/11/2011 – MORSI

I met this Cambodian family as they

Listen to the silent exchange of heartbeats and you will be forever grateful. I met this Cambodian family as they offered me a ride across the Tonle Sap in the middle of the night, having gotten lost on a far shore. As a photojournalist I have seen many hardships in people's lives, yet this meeting left me with a new friendship and I took the family to my heart as my own, providing health care and other necessities through the help of friends in Cambodia. There comes a point where imagination cannot perceive how a life can be. At that moment, the only answer is to engage!

—Mohammed Massoud Morsi

I am grateful for losing my way and
the angels who have helped me find
it again . . .

—Ceci Del Cid

Today I cannot express
myself with words.
—Diana Lyn Cote

I am grateful for Nature . . .

I am grateful for the Love found in Nature—for its gifts, inspiration, nourishment, infinite intelligence, and for providing truths for me to rediscover again and again that bring me closer to my highest self.

We are all Nature.

—Lisa Sobolewski

I am grateful for having learned the "art of seeing" and being able to record nature's endless wonders to share with others and the world. Life is a daily visual inspiration!

—Ingrid Mathews

I am grateful for
missed op...
that fuel...

I am grateful for missed opportunities
that fuel the imagination. For the
words never said, sometimes for
the better. For youthful inertia and
the immeasurable development it
fostered, useless as it then seemed.
And for the filter of memory that
softens the sharp edges and fits
together the puzzling pieces.
—Tom Piezzo

For the words never said
sometimes for the better

For youthful inertia
and the immeasurable dev
useless as it then seem

And for the filter of m
that softens the sharp
and fits together the

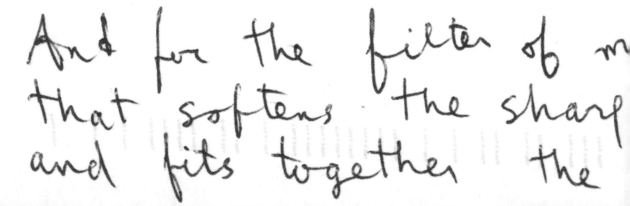

im grateful that sometimes the universe forces us to do things we are too afraid to try ourselves

—Wendy Natter

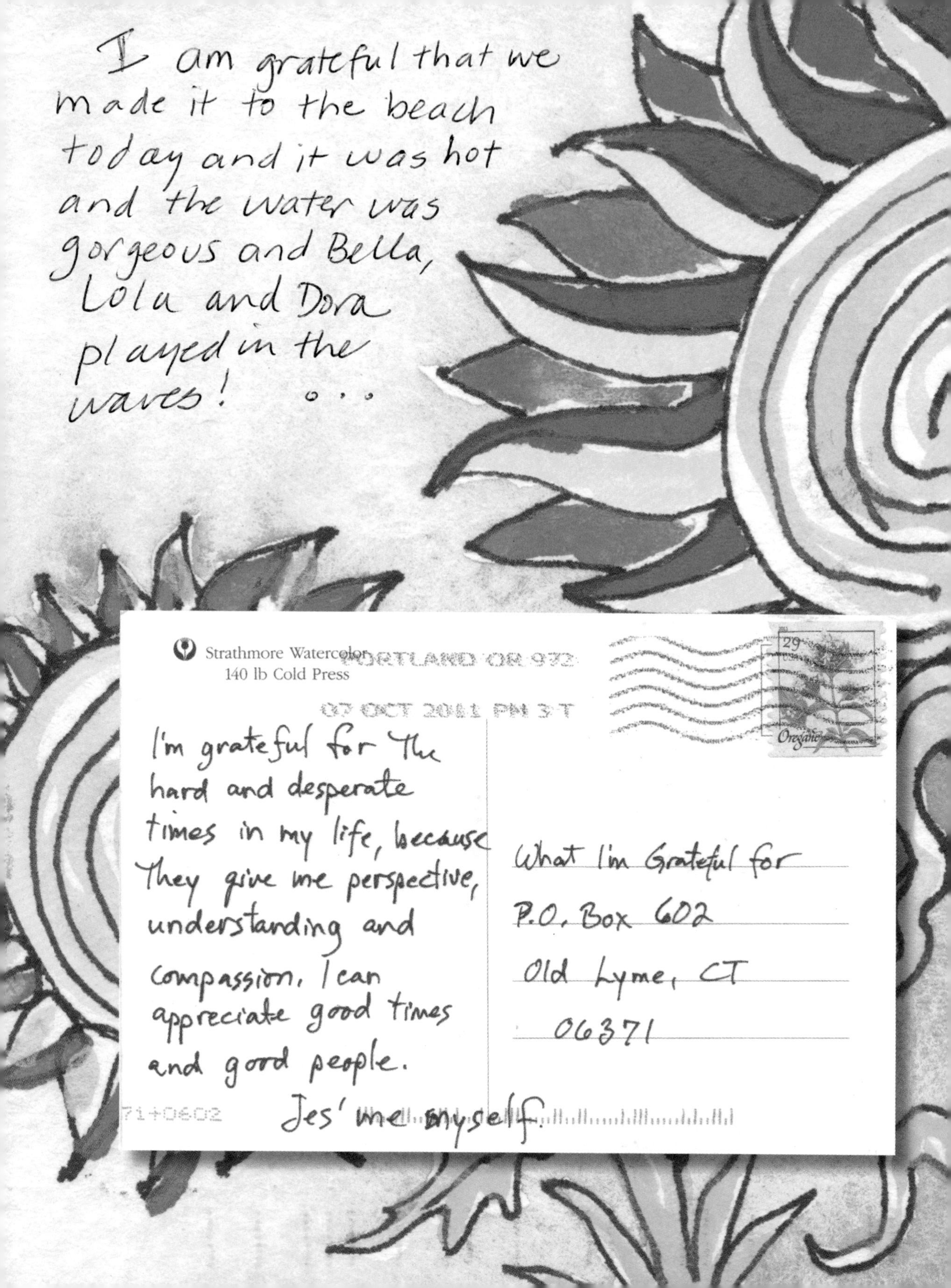

I am grateful that we made it to the beach today and it was hot and the water was gorgeous and Bella, Lola and Dora played in the waves! ○ ○ ○

Strathmore Watercolor
140 lb Cold Press

PORTLAND OR 972

07 OCT 2011 PM 3 T

29
Oregabic

I'm grateful for the hard and desperate times in my life, because they give me perspective, understanding and compassion. I can appreciate good times and good people.

Jes' me, myself.

What I'm Grateful for
P.O. Box 602
Old Lyme, CT
06371

71+0602

...I am also so grateful that I have had four perfect days at the beach with my favorite people in the world! Mom, Nicole, Mirabella, Lola and Isadora. We have all had time to talk, rest, read, eat, play and walk. Thank you, mom. I feel so lucky.

Rachel

At 91 Years Young,
I Am Grateful for The
wonderful world
around me, allowing
me To Live a Life
full of faith and love.

Alice W.

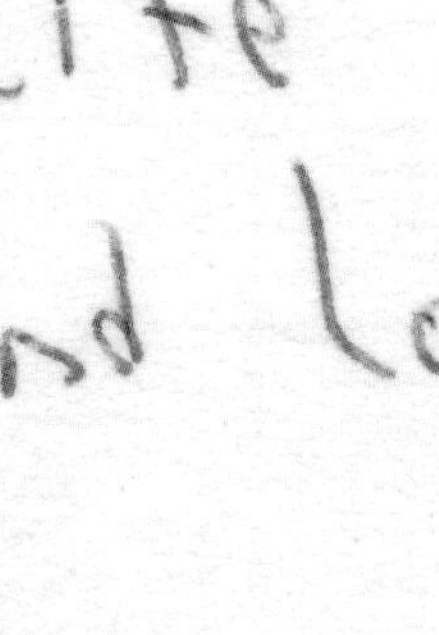

I am not insightful or quick of wit. It takes me time to come to conclusions because I like to think things through. So when I was asked what I was grateful for, I took some time to answer. And although a lot of things come to mind, what I keep coming back to is Wonder. In my personal, professional, and family life, I am grateful for a sense of wonder—the wonder of what will happen next; the wonder of how something new can inspire creativity; and the wonder of nature, which is the greatest gift of all. The sound of a wave, the feel of the wind—these are the things that make me stop and think. As a naturalist, I am grateful for being able to show children the wonders of nature and to see the excitement in their eyes.

I do not understand most of what happens in my life and I can't help but wonder what will happen next . . . but the fact that I don't know what will happen next keeps my eyes open to the possibilities.

—Ranger Russ Miller

July 19, 2014

I am deeply grateful for my beautiful daughters & granddaughters me, as I love God... This is a perfect page for of wonder and am at this moment sitting outside of the little Sunkist cottage in Monsook

All morning spent on a spectacular sunny blue skied ocean — the grand girls Nurdhella, Isolera Yola standing at Oceans edge running wildly back to the waves break.

UTTERLY, emotionally moments of wonderment, gratitude and love of my family of women & girls growing to women and also of my God, His love of me & my love of Him.

Image by Fred Marotti

I'm grateful for **courage**

Open your eyes to your own potential. When you catch a glimpse of the strength inside, your courage is unleashed.

You are greater than you think.

—AOK

"And the day came when the risk to remain tight in a bud was more painful than the risk it took to blossom."

—Anaïs Nin

Olympian Sarah Trowbridge writes:

When I was nine, I wrote in my diary; "I decided I am going to be an Olympian today." Although I promptly followed it up with a list of the boys I had crushes on, the priority was clear and I was sure of myself.

In 2005, I was a relatively successful college rower, but not the best in the country, or even on my university rowing team. In general, I was a good technical rower, despite being short, but was lacking a certain amount of power over long distances. I was always just shy of "great" on rowing tests but made up for it with my skill and ferocity in races.

Despite any shortcomings, I was very confident that I could not only hold my own, but could actually best other rowers. That's why, when I had some success in college and felt like I still had further to go, I decided to try for the US National Rowing Team. I was certain that I could be an Olympian and would be a great addition to the group, but I had the uphill battle of not being the ideal candidate. Again, I was short and not the best at long distance.

In 2007, I made my first national team: the Pan-American Team. Although this wasn't the top tier national team to make, my doubles partner and I did really well and I felt like I had made progress. The next year, 2008, I was just shy of the Olympic team and, instead, made the World Championships.

My foot was in the door! But it was clear that I still had a lot to do to make the 2012 US Olympic Team. I was told "No" on a monthly basis and it usually came down to my weaknesses in endurance. The more I improved on my weakness, the more my teammates improved too.

Through shear determination, I clawed my way up the ranks and, in 2009, made my first major national team and even won a silver medal at the World Championships.

I was on a roll!

Every year I struggled to improve but, by the end of the year, I came through and got a little closer to my Olympic dreams. By 2011, I felt like I was one of the fastest rowers in sculling and was beyond fired up with motivation from my progress. I felt unstoppable.

I was certain I could make history in my sport and, furthermore, find validation that all the hardships were worth it. After years of underappreciation by my coaches, lack of a consistent salary, and sacrifices of "normal life" benchmarks that my peers held paramount, I was ready to make the most of it. If someone asked me to do an eighty-minute workout, I would do one hundred minutes; if I had a free Sunday afternoon, I would go for an extra run.

But that's when I was cut from the team. Despite my best efforts and extra training, I fell short on an endurance test in December 2011. My team left for a winter training camp and I moved out of my apartment. I felt singled out, ashamed, and helpless.

Over my twelve-year career as a rower, I had experienced many setbacks. I had been so frustrated I wanted to quit, cry, throw punches, or crawl into a hole to forget my dream altogether. But this was the biggest blow ever. I had so much pride in what I was doing. I had made five national teams; I had gotten to visit countries like Brazil and New Zealand representing my country; I had won the first medal at a World Championship in the US women's quad event; and I had gotten that far because I was tough and disciplined. How could this happen? After overcoming so many challenges, I deserved to make the Olympic team because I hadn't had it easy.

In the first couple of months after being cut, I was so busy being angry that it never occurred to me how self-righteous I had become. I was so confused about what I should do. Although it would have been easy to walk away at that point, I just couldn't let go. Despite my confusion and anger—or maybe because of it—I was determined to find a new route to the Olympics, now just eight months away.

And as I began to pick up the pieces, I found myself rowing at the Potomac Boat Club, the first place I rowed after college. I decided to row with another sculler who had also had a lot of success followed by some major setbacks and we chose a fantastic coach.

But despite our best efforts, we came to the April trials unprepared. To move closer to the Olympic Games, we needed to place first, but instead came in third. And in a moment, the story was over and my nine-year-old diary closed. Suddenly, I saw where my pride had gotten in the way and how my grudges had weighed me down. I realized that just because I had been successful in the past and had sometimes had things harder than others, it didn't mean that I would always be successful or deserve anything more than anyone else. My regret was palpable.

But thankfully, one hour after this painful defeat, we received a phone call.

The two boats that beat us were declining the Olympic doubles spot to go for another event. And so we were suddenly back in the game!

Some moments just put things in perspective.

—Diana Lyn Cote

My partner and I vowed to make the most of this rare opportunity. We did a complete overhaul of our training efforts and, most important, our mentality. In those few months leading up to the Olympics, I forced myself to accurately identify my strengths and weaknesses and to trust them. I also turned off the voice that said, "I'll show you, just wait," because it wasn't allowing me to make the necessary changes to be a true Olympian. Little by little, I began to respect my shortcomings, trust my strengths, and step over my pride. It was a time of hard work and humility.

In May 2012, at the Olympic Qualification Regatta in Lucerne, Switzerland, my partner and I came in first place—stamping our ticket to London just nine weeks before the opening ceremonies.

Without the setbacks, I would not appreciate where I am today, and without the found humility, I would not have as deep of a love for the entire experience. I am so proud to be an Olympian, but even more grateful to have had a chance to participate, to stand next to my teammates, and to respect my competition.

I am grateful to my parents who taught me to dream. I am grateful for my friends who shared my dreams. I am grateful for my wife who supported my dreams. Finally, I am grateful for my daughter who helped me realize my dreams.

—Partha Pratim Ghosh

How are you finding courage in *your* life?

What does courage mean to you? Why does courage make you grateful?

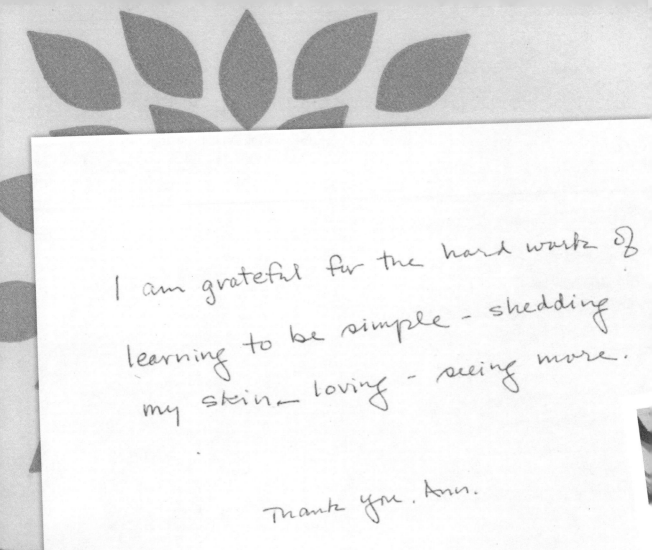

I am grateful for the hard work of learning to be simple - shedding my skin - loving - seeing more.

Thank you, Ann.

Twelve-year Alcoholics Anonymous sobriety medallion submitted by an anonymous participant.

am grateful for

HOPE

—Laura Kaiser

פליט

Looking To a Brighter Future

Very Thankful!

—Annie Hardy

People tell me I'm strong.

When my daughter had a stroke, I did not fall apart. I asked for help and found support in many ways so that I could rise above the fear, the denial, and the grief.

There were decisions to be made and I had to be able to balance the fierce love for my daughter with the medical facts.

What I discovered was that facts were not what guided me, but an unswerving clarity that I could understand my daughter's wishes—unspoken—through my love for her and some other mystical understanding.

When the doctors said to let her go, that she would never progress beyond a persistent vegetative state, I fought on, with a mixture of hope, grief, and despair.

Not a happy ending, because my daughter is still unmoving and silent. But today she can say "yes" by moving her eye.

—Nancy Smith Worthen*
See page 140 for image of Nancy and her daughter.

I'm grateful for people who see with their hearts.

—Donna Marie Joyce, Esq.

In this year of thankfulness,
I recognize struggle, and
those doing their best.

—Diana Lyn Cote

제가 세상의
반대쪽으로
이사 했는데도
불구 하고
사랑 하는
가족들은
저를
따뜻하게
받아들였습니다.

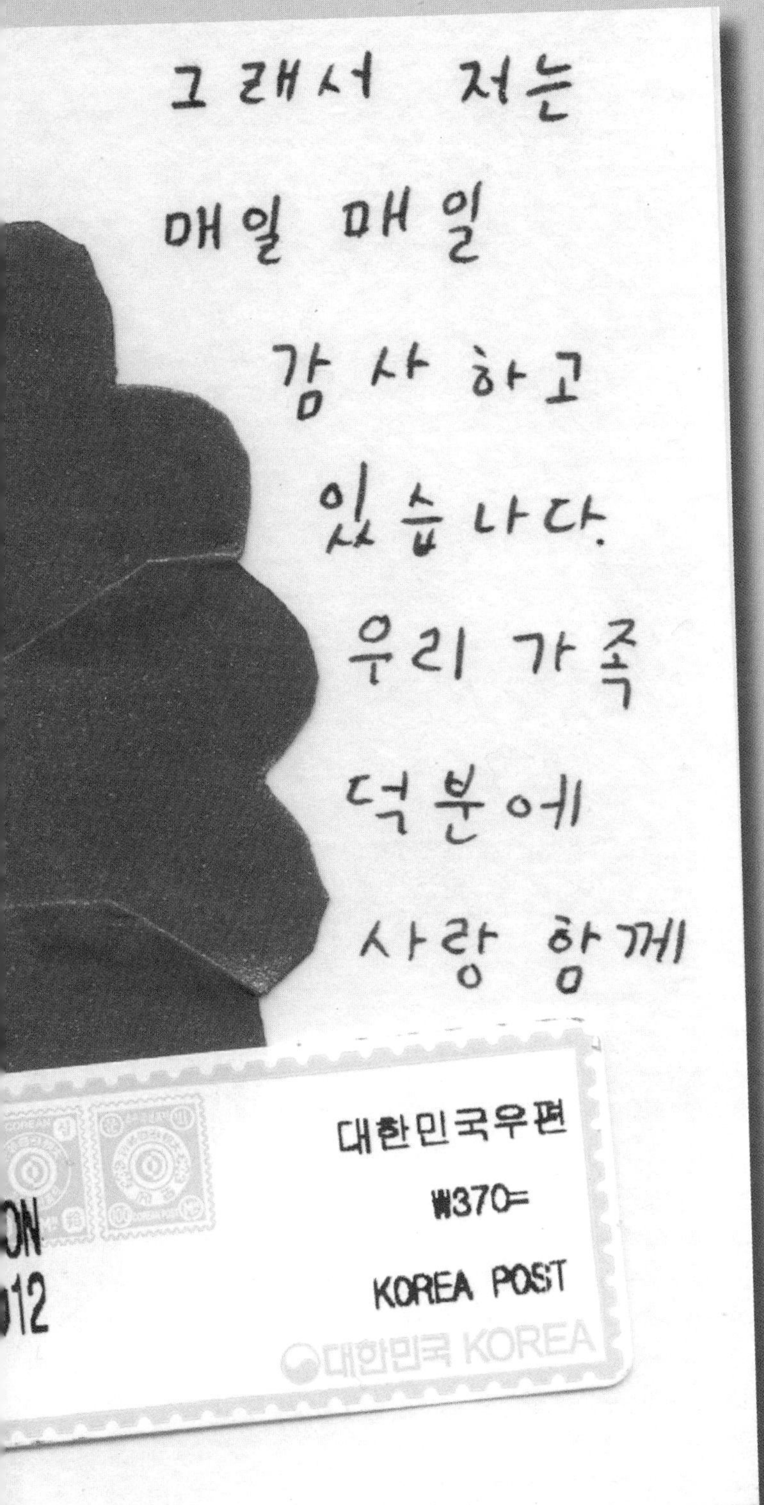

그래서 저는

매일 매일

감사하고

있습니다.

우리 가족

덕분에

사랑 함께

대한민국우편

₩370=

KOREA POST

대한민국 KOREA

Translation: Although I moved to the other side of the world, a loving family has warmly accepted me into their lives. So, I am thankful every day. Thanks to my family, I am able to live with love.

—Elena Lee

love and possibilities...

jahre radio-schweiz
ans radio-suisse
anni radio-suisse

I am grateful to the mother who 64 years ago had the strength to put me up for adoption, thus giving me the most wonderful life and family. I wonder if she thinks of me as often as I think of her, and I hope her life went on to be as rich as mine.

—Anonymous

I have made a lot of mistakes and am going to continue making them. But that's why I'm motivated to keep moving forward. From your mistakes, take the best and convert it into something positive. When we achieve that spirit of oneness . . . we are going to achieve things that we could never imagine.

—Julio S.
Sea turtle poacher turned conservationist

This image of a loggerhead sea turtle was taken on a Mexican fishing boat, twenty miles offshore by sea turtle biologist Jesse Senko.

I am thankful for my experiences good and bad, the moon that shines keeping the darkness away, the leaves that give us hope, and the laughter that fills our hearts.

—Jordan Fox

In a few hours I'll be boarding a flight home to New York City, but for the past ten days I've felt completely at "home" visiting Lily of the Valley, a children's orphanage in KwaZulu-Natal, South Africa. The experience I've just had is one that is hard to put into words, for words could never explain the way these children have changed not only my life, but, more important, my heart. These children, most of whom are HIV-positive from birth, are the most courageous and God-loving people I've ever had the privilege of knowing, despite having so little. In just ten short days, they have shown me so much love in its purest form. You ask me what I'm thankful for. I thank God for these children, full of love and hope, who are capable of changing this world one heart, one life, at a time.

—Melissa Markle

Image by Diana Lyn Cote

Thought comes to mind, "Look for the Good." It is everywhere, timeless, and in all things so we may realize it anywhere, anytime. It lives immutably in our consciousness.

The Bad also exists and informs our search but can affect only our daily life and its finite activity. We do not have to look for the Bad—it arrives and departs on its own.

The Good and the Bad weave together, and may even appear similar. But only the Good endures. Each time, thought comes to mind and we look for it, the Good and our souls become one.

—Fred Osborne

I'm grateful for **grace**

When you leap wholeheartedly into the present moment, grace appears. Surrender to the gentle promptings of your own heart. Wherever love leads, grace follows.

Grace is evidence of love.

—AOK

"Grace is uncovering the sweet nectar of your one true identity and then going on to see it in everything and everyone around you."

—Karianna Rosenberg

Naturalist Karianna Rosenberg writes:

Grace, for me, is gratitude for everything in life—as life itself is a gift. Grace is harmony, fluidity, and circles. Grace flows and has soft music. Grace can make one's heart sing. Grace is all around us: It is in a mountain's shape, in the sculptural quality of a tree, in the bounding of a deer, in a hop of a mouse, or the soaring of an eagle. Grace is also nurturing and caring, like a mother's love for her child. It is the curved lines and soft movements of dance; a smile; the honey sweetness of a lover's embrace; and the aroma of a flower. Grace is the gentle warmth of a sunrise; the kind, outreached hand of a friend; the ebb and flow of the tides; and the silver-blue light of the moon. To walk with grace is to walk with gratitude in one's heart, and to see and experience the world with love.

I have come to understand how much life itself is a grace ever since I experienced two severe injuries in my twenties. I was struck by lightning twice—both times, indoors—two years apart. More than half my body was fried from internal burns. I acquired a traumatic brain injury, which resulted in short-term memory loss for over a year, among other difficulties that persisted for many more years. I had to relearn to walk, which was very difficult emotionally as I am a dancer and dance is one of my greatest passions. Severe pain, headache, and muscle aches were with me daily. I was fully aware of what I had been able to do before, so the process of relearning was tremendously frustrating.

It was a very slow and powerful journey of healing—physically, emotionally, and spiritually. I believe the deep determination that pushed through me to heal and truly live again was a grace. I am dancing again and can say I am 120 percent me—fully healed! The night of my first strike, I knew it was a gift and that I'd be learning from it for many years to come. I have always embraced both lightning strikes as gifts and consider them my other two birthdays.

As part of my journey, I had several near-death experiences. Once one crosses over and returns, one's perspective is forever changed. I believe just being alive is a grace. Life is so precious. Every moment is precious and every thing around us is too. Embracing life with grace is so important, but to remember that life itself is a grace is even more important.

My healing journey has brought me in touch with many indigenous cultures from around the world. Through the individuals I've met, I've learned to live mindfully and "heartfully" and understand this on a deep level. I am so sensitive to all that is around me, it is almost as if the lightning blew open a portal in my being. Having the tremendous power of lightning—a bridge between earth and sky—pulse through me, I have come to know intimately how intrinsically we are connected to all life around us.

Through this deepened connection, I have learned to consciously acknowledge life with a grateful heart. Greeting the sun each morning, I connect with each of the elements: earth, air, fire, and water. We can so easily take them for granted yet they are what give us life. I greet them with gratitude: A firm and nurturing earth to stand upon; the gift of breath we exchange with plants; the fiery warmth of the sun that echoes the fire within each of our hearts; and fluid water, the liquid essence of life. I acknowledge each element and its qualities so that I can feel them around me and swirling within my very being. I awaken each of my senses to the land around me, acknowledging that I am part of the land, and the land is part of me. To live with grace is to fully appreciate and understand that life is precious, all forms of life are grace, and all life is sacred.

How are you finding grace in *your* life?

What does grace mean to you? Why does grace make you grateful?

7/25/19 I woke up this morning and chose "GRACE" - wanted to write - but we were on our way out the door. Now - sitting outside no picnic table

I love her line "I am so sensitive to all that is around me; it is almost as if the lightening blew open a portal in my being".

Grace comes to me & flows through me through a portal at the top of my head (being) & gushes powerfully in the most beautiful silvers - whites, irredescent tones. I ask God for His Grace every day to help me have wisdom, love, serenity and focus on my purpose and path given to me by God. It is the greatest gift imaginable - abundant - everflowing -

Grace is the Source - it is all & everything. It empowers - Lights - gives my eyes a perspective of love, gratitude (deep, deep gratitude) for all that life is

Grace is my birthright (and yours) that connects us like an umbilical cord from our God, our Source, our universe. It took me over 1/2 my life to feel the Truth of it and to understand I am forgiven for all my humanness and deserve and am worthy of God's love and that my path is to light up others to see and feel their worth. Although I have always been a seeker - my sister, Nancy's death, february 27, 2012 - changed me & accelerated my spiritual path. Nancy's greatest gift to me "we have to

181

have FAITH, Eight? Right. She passed to God's arms the next day

In 1978 when I enlisted in the navy, I was about to go to the airport where I wouldn't see my mom for another nine months to a year. She came to me before I left and she had this little article that she had cut out from the *Hartford Courant.* She said, "If you could live your life by what is in this article, I'd be really proud of you." I've kept this article with me since then. As you can see, it's pretty deteriorated, but I never wanted to lose the words. So about ten years ago I retyped it and laminated it so that I could carry it with me all the time. I'm grateful for my mom because she was the epitome of kindness. She never had a bad word to say about anyone. Regardless of what people did to her, she always found the silver lining. My dad lost his eyesight when he was forty-five and unfortunately became a pretty bad alcoholic after that. My mom took a lot of punches for us . . . He was a pretty violent guy, but she was never afraid of standing up and taking the heat for us. She always had the courage to stand up for what was right, and I always admired her for that. I try to do that on a small scale, but I can't compare it to what she did.

—Henry Alves

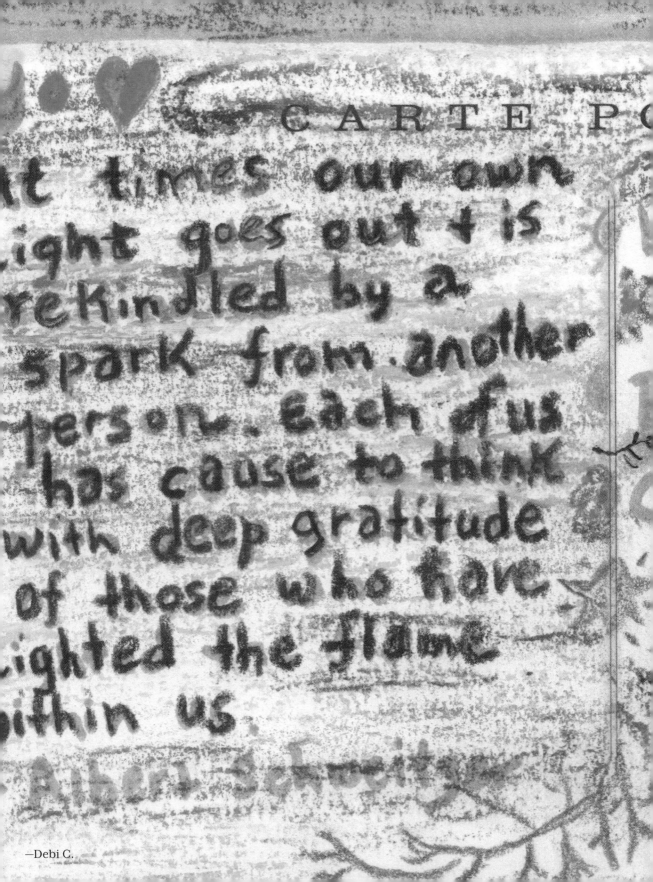

At times our own light goes out + is rekindled by a spark from another person. each of us has cause to think with deep gratitude of those who have lighted the flame within us

— Albert Schweitzer

—Debi C.

Today on the drive home . . . I found myself thinking angry thoughts about a couple of folks . . . driving like jerks. To put myself in a better mood, I pulled off at a rest stop to get some pistachios. As if that weren't reward enough in its own right, on the way into the store, I smiled at a little girl (about nine years old) and she responded by giving this little skip and flourish with her arms wide open as she smiled back as if to say, "Tada! Aren't we lucky to be here?" It was fabulous, and made me a little grateful for the jerks on the road who inspired me to stop.

—Robert Messore

Julia Farrand Age 4

Dear Anne,

I am grateful for the way someone appears with a kind word, just at the right time.

—Anonymous

I'm thankful for my sister saving my life by making me stop choking

—Corbin H.

What I am grateful for:

Recently, both my parents passed away. I am grateful that I was able to be with both of them at the end despite living in another state. It was as if they waited for me...

—Denis

Gratitude is my life's work. It has changed my life.

—Jody Prusi

Nhean is my neighbour. He supports his family by driving people around Phnom Penh [Cambodia] on a Moto . . . The first time I met Nhean, he was sitting outside his home. He smoked a cigarette and dipped a green mango in chili as he watched his kids play . . . In reality, I don't speak Khmer well enough to communicate with Nhean. However, we are good friends now. He's plucking a duck here, his daughter helping him. We are both smiling.

—Mohammed Massoud Morsi

I'm grateful for my dad who built a boat with me. It is good to work together, especially if you didn't know that you could.

—Anonymous

Something called me to the lake that golden autumn afternoon. Surrendering to a compelling desire to be in my kayak, I was soon sliding into the water, my oar entering the rhythm of waves. A strong headwind forced me to reverse my usual course and retreat into a protected cove.

Noticing fine white feathers on the water, I followed a narrow channel overgrown with berry-red vines trailing down to the water. Paddling through a maze of tall grasses, I turned into a hidden inlet and suddenly came upon a family of swan—male, female, and signet. All startled, we froze.

Hoping to prevent their imminent flight, I sent silent greetings of benign intent, and gradually, the swan returned to their preening and nuzzling. As the gentle current drew me closer, the female swan started to swim, followed by the signet, with the male guarding the rear. Paddling ever so subtly, I became the fourth swan, gliding over the water in a slow graceful dance until I came a bit too close, invading the male's comfort zone. Ever so slightly, he raised his wings to broaden his stance, and just in this moment, the saturated afternoon sun bathed his downy back in translucent light. Instantly, I knew what had beaconed me to the lake —God's kiss, beauty's eternal embrace.

I followed in reverence until we arrived back at the opening of the cove. Then, the male swan swam to the side and gestured me to pass. Knowing I had received a rare gift, I didn't look back. Awed by this divine encounter I returned home just in time to teach my cello student Saint Saens' *The Swan*—with transcendent understanding.

—Ann West

Images on both pages by Diana Lyn Cote

I AM GRATEFULL FOR THE

POETRY of TIME

David Allen

I'm grateful for my sister Ann's humor and grace following the recent loss of both her legs due to spinal meningitis and total septic shock. I am constantly amazed at her love of life and those who love her, in spite of extremely trying circumstances. She is someone who has always looked for the good in others and in life, and so steadfastly remains. If such gratitude exists for someone whom life has treated so harshly, then who am I to complain of anything at all?

—David

Upon returning on 9.21.2005 after evacuating for [Hurricane] Katrina, in bloom in my yard this flower: a moment of pure joy.

—Suzon E.

The seasons change. The footprints change. Even the boards get changed. The path remains.

—Diana Lyn Cote

I'm grateful for joy

Joy is pure sunshine pressed into life. It is in the birds calling excitedly at dawn . . . a cat curled in the sun . . . a baby laughing with glee. Joy is simple, pure, and unadulterated. And because gratitude lifts our eyes to the horizon, what are *you* grateful for today? In this moment, find the joy.

—AOK

Image by Lisa Sobolewski

"It is not joy that makes us grateful. It is gratitude that makes us joyful."

— Brother David Steindl-Rast

Librarian Tom Piezzo shares:

Joy. At some past point, all it took was a crayon and a glass of chocolate milk. The entirety of my existence culminated in that moment and my rapture was unbound. Then I got "smarter" and learned how to see the gray. Joy was reduced to a motto emblazoned on a Christmas ornament. There were glad moments of course, but, perversely, these were alloyed with grudges and doubts. Puberty sucked, for example.

After I stopped trying to be too cool to be impressed, which is to say, being too frightened to trust and allow anything to reach me, things came to rather a dull pass . . . for years.

But recently, my joy has come back. Maybe it was when I saw a three-year-old positively levitate in delight over a passing fire truck. Or, when I saw a panting dog rolling itself into a tamale of twigs and dirt. But however it started, the joy was back, simply because I let it in.

The small daily joys accrue to leaven life, and relieve the nagging expectation for larger ones. And as I reflect more about my childhood love of crayons and chocolate milk, I recall I was motivated to draw my misshapen portraits because my grandma seemed so thrilled to get them. It was a mutually happy experience—and was always punctuated with a glass of chocolate milk! So joy comes in many ways.

It's the sudden yellow and orange of April, the exaltation of reaching the mountaintop, or the perfectly turned sestina. It's watching the dozing infant, or being the old dancing fool who won't act his age. It is every morning the T cells are good, and every morning that they're not, because you're still awake and alive and able to enjoy the day. It's winning the pennant, or not caring to keep score as you play. It's the quiet satisfaction of the comforting routine that awaits you day after day or, conversely, the ecstatic, hectic immersion when you forget the time and don't hear the phone ringing. These are the joys you create, maybe later to abandon or replace or build upon. But in between the factoids and the crises, joy is still waiting.

"A curved slice of sunshine straight off the tree."

—Diana Lyn Cote

How are you finding joy in *your* life?

What does joy mean to you? Why does joy make you grateful?

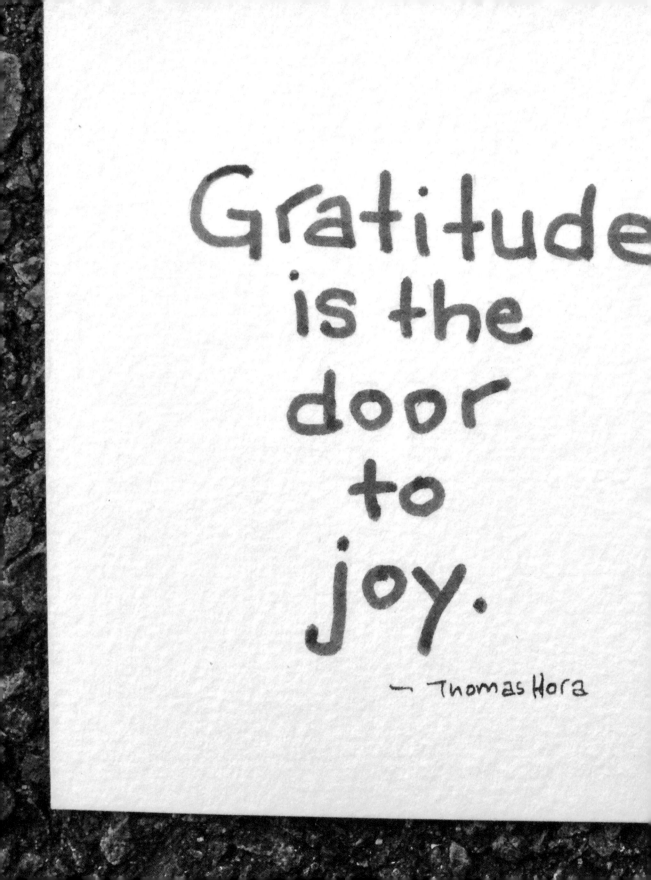

Gratitude
is the
door
to
joy.

— Thomas Hora

ON THE BACK: I am grateful for the ability to discern beauty, love, order, harmony, and all spiritual qualities.

—Heather Brodhead

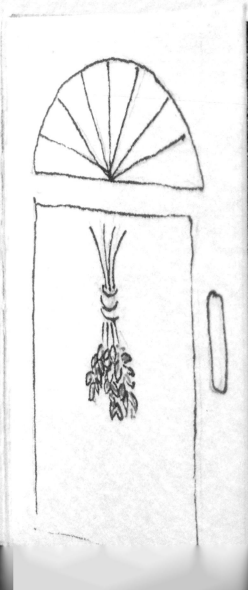

MY
DOG PEES
FROM JOY
WHEN I COME
HOME

—Evgeny Bam

TOP: *Darwin;* MIDDLE:
Joan; BOTTOM: *Lucky*

MY FAVORITE THINGS

The reddish and purpelish mountains of La Paz

The scent of jasmines, coffee trees and citrus

Warm morning greetings from my hubby

The majesty and magic of The ocean

The voice of my grandma

The Sound of MUSIC

My mama's hands

Fluffy bunnies

Carrot Cake

XIMENA
LA PAZ, BOLIVIA

I'm grateful for the world

I'm greatful for the sky

Gabrie
La Paz, B

I'm grateful for being part of our family crew

I'm greatful for yo
canyon-lips, always loa
and ready to fire kisses

I'm grateful I can travel the world on your smile

I'm grateful for the ocean

I'm gratefu
for the
fish

Gabriel   Ximena

Ximena writes:

I'm grateful for the many blessings, for the beauty of "small things," the pleasures of everyday life, the majesty of nature, and the endless love of my family and friends. [These are] my favorite things: The reddish and purplish mountains of La Paz; the scent of jasmines, coffee trees, and citrus; warm morning greetings from my hubby; the majesty and magic of the ocean; the voice of my grandma; the sound of music; my mama's hands; fluffy bunnies; [and] carrot cake.

Inspired by his wife, Gabriel then writes:

I'm grateful for the world; I'm grateful for being part of our family crew; I'm grateful I can travel the world on your smile; I'm grateful for the ocean; I'm grateful for the fish; I'm grateful for the sky; I'm grateful for your canyon-lips, always loaded and ready to fire kisses.

LOOK for the GOOD
CAN YOU see it?

JOY . . . ART . . . COLOR

gratitude for COLOR!

—Julie Eberle

I am grateful for the sheer resilience of the human spirit, that even after enduring great loss we are able to heal and experience joy, warmth, and love.

—Zohra

Mama to baby boy Ammar (born November 2012) and an angel baby (lost May 2011)

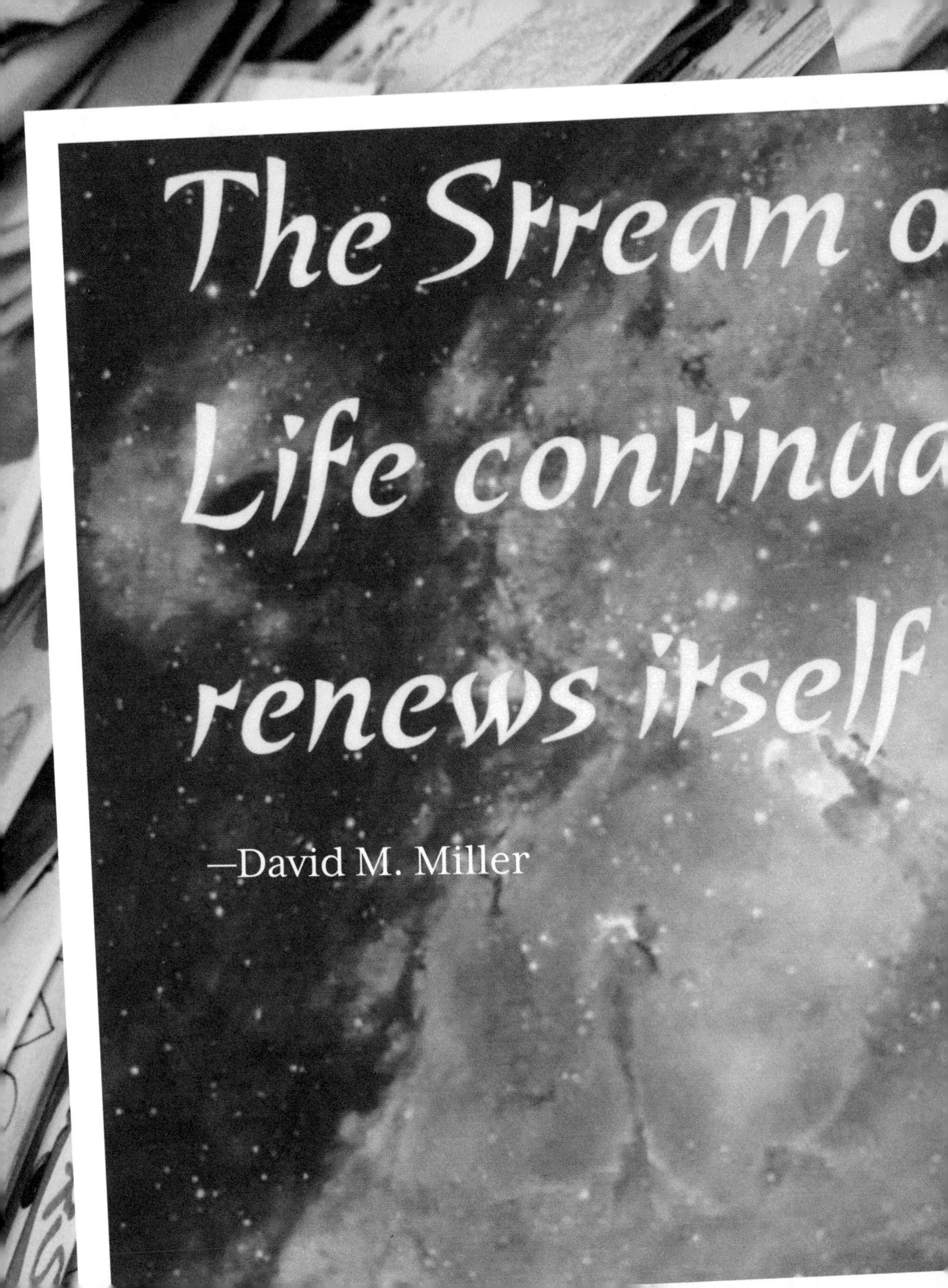

The Stream o

Life continua

renews itself

—David M. Miller

My heart is filled with gratitude for music and for the blessed opportunity that singing has offered me to glimpse the hidden Perfection of the Divine, bursting into our world through the sacred gift that music is. We have only to be still to hear this music break forth through the songbirds that tweet, the geese that honk, the crickets that chirp, the frogs that croak, the owls that hoot, the elephants that trumpet, the whales that click, and the penguins that peep—these "performers" are all expressing the One Eternal Song, communicating Joy in Existence and freely celebrating Life! Stay tuned and listen for the Good!

—Susan von Reichenbach

Thank you for our colorful WORLD!

—Vladimir Shpitalnik

I am so grateful to have such a big, wonderful world to explore! I love to have adventures! I love to have so much fun! I am so grateful to have a sister! I love to spend time with my best friend. I love to play, to love art, and to create. I love to have such a nice life! I love to have such a wonderful, grateful life!

THANK YOU

What Makes me Grateful is
my mom, cousins, faimly, friends
pets and the bEACH!

— Isadore

I am 3

And This second

I am grateful for my life and this is my faimly I love this

Ellie/Dej in: M

Image by Diana Lyn Cote

My gratitude list is as fluid as water finding its way along a rocky creek bed. That may be what drew me to your project, the all-encompassing, fluid nature of it all . . . I still wake up some days with ideas for postcards. I haven't been very good about following through on them, however. Maybe today . . .

—Jyoti

Beautiful

grateful for?

LOIA

Photo by Abrien Broom

Can't think of anything?

Then just remember . . .

you are AMAZING!

life   love   beauty   health   peace   freedom

Photo by Lisa Sobolewski

> When you look for the good, it grows... and the first place it blooms is in YOU. Do you see it?

Deep down, these qualities are within you and available to enrich your life. All you have to do to cultivate them is appreciate them. When you look for the good, it grows . . . and the first place it blooms is in *you.*

Do you see it?

Good begins with gratitude!

creativity   abundance   insight   courage   grace   joy

PARTICIPATE!

You are invited to write or draw a glimmer of gladness on
a postcard-sized anything and mail it to:

WHAT I'M GRATEFUL FOR
PO BOX 602
Old Lyme, CT 06371
USA

Don't worry, stick figures are perfectly
acceptable, and you don't have to be an artist to participate.

To see more postcards or to find out if your card made it onto the web, check out

lookforthegoodproject.org.

A GAME

If you don't want to fill out a postcard, that's OK, because this project isn't really about postcards. It's about the quality of your presence every time you take a moment to choose gratitude. So here's a little game you can play instead.

1. Take this book into a public space, like a coffee shop.

2. Sit down at a table.

3. Close the book with the back cover facing up. (You might notice that there's an arrow on the back.)

4. Then spin the book. Yes, you read that correctly—spin the book like you might spin a bottle.

5. Then watch the arrow. Where is it pointing? See if you can find the good in whomever happens to be nearby. Can you see love? Kindness? Generosity? Strength? Creativity? Humor? Take the time to appreciate the person.

6. If you're feeling adventurous, cut out a card from the page opposite and give it to the person. And then, for the most important part: High-five and make a new friend.

. . . I dare you! :−)

{ I'm grateful for your presence }   { I'm grateful for your presence }   { I'm grateful for your presence }

{ I'm grateful for your presence }   { I'm grateful for your presence }   { I'm grateful for your presence }

{ I'm grateful for your presence }   { I'm grateful for your presence }   { I'm grateful for your presence }

You've been given this card because your presence is appreciated. Please pass this on when you see the good in someone too.

———

What Makes YOU Grateful?
lookforthegoodproject.org

You've been given this card because your presence is appreciated. Please pass this on when you see the good in someone too.

———

What Makes YOU Grateful?
lookforthegoodproject.org

You've been given this card because your presence is appreciated. Please pass this on when you see the good in someone too.

———

What Makes YOU Grateful?
lookforthegoodproject.org

You've been given this card because your presence is appreciated. Please pass this on when you see the good in someone too.

———

What Makes YOU Grateful?
lookforthegoodproject.org

You've been given this card because your presence is appreciated. Please pass this on when you see the good in someone too.

———

What Makes YOU Grateful?
lookforthegoodproject.org

You've been given this card because your presence is appreciated. Please pass this on when you see the good in someone too.

———

What Makes YOU Grateful?
lookforthegoodproject.org

You've been given this card because your presence is appreciated. Please pass this on when you see the good in someone too.

———

What Makes YOU Grateful?
lookforthegoodproject.org

You've been given this card because your presence is appreciated. Please pass this on when you see the good in someone too.

———

What Makes YOU Grateful?
lookforthegoodproject.org

You've been given this card because your presence is appreciated. Please pass this on when you see the good in someone too.

———

What Makes YOU Grateful?
lookforthegoodproject.org

SOME EXTRA TIPS

"You don't have to see the whole staircase, just take the first step."
—Martin Luther King Jr.

Remember, gratitude can be hard work. That's why Drs. Jeffrey F. Froh and Robert Emmons suggest a few other ways to keep your gratitude going:

☐ Keep a Gratitude Journal

☐ Find a "Gratitude Accountability Buddy" (someone who will check up on whether or not you're looking for the good)

☐ Watch Your Language

☐ Pause Mindfully

☐ Savor Good Times

☐ Count Your Blessings

☐ Don't Be Afraid to Remember Pain

THANKS!

I am so grateful to the thousands of people who have already participated in this project. If you are one of them, your postcard has served to brighten my day, inspire my work, and heal my life. And for this, I am forever grateful. I'd also like to thank the many people who donated to the project in some way, shape, or form:

ANGELS: Birch Bidwell; Katie Bryant; Jill Butler; Jim and Marianne Cassidy; Elizabeth Cook; Gary DeMichele; Betsy Devany; Bob and Jean Draggon; Alaina Driscoll; Jim and Jeffrey Enderle; Khristy Ferguson; Brian Foley; Keith Fox; John and Debi Friedlander; Sarah Smith Gerritz; Trevor Giles; Debbie Goodrow; Bob Grills; Frank Grundman; Suellen Heinrich; Tony Hurtado; Mathew Ingraham; Elliott C. Johnson; Patte Leathe; John Littel and Brian DelCavo; Lori Mack; Emily Malpino; Dara, Troy, and McKenna Marino; Pam Stevens Moriarty; Wendy Natter; Sarah Drought Nebel; Stuart Pearl; Mary Pendergast; Coleen and Larry Proctor; Julie Reiten; Marilyn Searle; Aileen Shen; Vladimir Shpitalnik; Sisters of Mercy; and Susan von Reichenbach.

SUPER ANGELS: Nick and Marilyn Boretz; Marshall Clark; Patty and Wayne Devoe; Noah Kaeser; Dr. Timothy McLaughlin; Mohammed Massoud Morsi; Fred and Judith Barbour Osborne; Janet Toenjes; and Jerry Weiss.

AMAZINGLY AWESOME ANGELS: Chris Zane, Zane's Cycles, and the Zane Foundation; Trailblazer; R.J. Julia Booksellers; Reclamation Lumber; the Friends of Hammonasset; Russ Miller, Henry Alves, and all the folks at the Meigs Point Nature Center and Hammonasset Beach State Park; G-Zen Restaurant; Pamela and Ted Hamilton; Samantha MacRae Foerster, Tevis Trower, and Balance Integration Corporation; Heather Brodhead; Lorre Broom; Marjorie and Dave Colton; Claire; Jyoti Kenney; Matt and Irene Kubitsky; Questa Builders, Inc.; Ruth Robins; Marc Scrivener; the Sparkle Fairy; Sarita Van Vlek; Patti Anne Vassia; and Martin and Joanne Varley.

In addition, I'd like to thank the many dogs, cats, horses, chickens, and fish who generously shared their homes with me while their owners were away (thank you, pet owners, for inviting me to stay!); my parents for lovingly housing me when I had no place else to go; Diana Lyn Cote, whose 366 postcard paintings inspired me day after day and gave me the courage to keep going when things were tough; Edna and Doug Noiles, whose kindness and generosity never ceases to astound me; the media, who gave the project air time, column space, or precious glossy pages; Faith Middleton of WNPR for helping me raise money on the air, even though she was not feeling well the day of our first interview; Mary Norris for believing in me and all the talented folks at Globe Pequot Press for helping me create this book; my agent, Esmond Harmsworth, for his generosity and kindness; the many nameless people who spontaneously donated money, food, clothing, advice, housing, services, or energy when I told them about the project; Briana Levine for first pointing out the joys of postcard art; Frank Warren of PostSecret, who took the time to encourage and inspire me while visiting my small state; Vladimir and Anna Shpitalnik for helping me in so many ways; the many libraries, schools, organizations, and individuals worldwide who helped me spread the word; Smith College and its amazing staff and alums; Sean Callinan, Samantha MacRae Foerster, Marc Scrivener, Jesse Senko, Seth Bannon, Katherine Thompson, and Russ Miller for moral support; Birch Bidwell, Valery Shevchenko, and Serge Shevchenko for their photo and computer support; Doe Boyle and the Shoreline Arts Alliance; Judith Barbour Osborne, Keith Fox, Noah Kaeser, Trevor Giles, Debi and John Friedlander, Bill LaRoue, PhD, Rachel Perry, and so many others who helped me with the first exhibition; Jack and Sosse Baker of the Chester Gallery; the New London Maritime Museum, the Provenance Center, Mercy Center, Hammonasset Beach State Park, the Pond House, and the Zen Mountain Monastery; YOU for reading this book; and all the people who continue to participate in this project. YOU have helped give voice to gratitude . . .

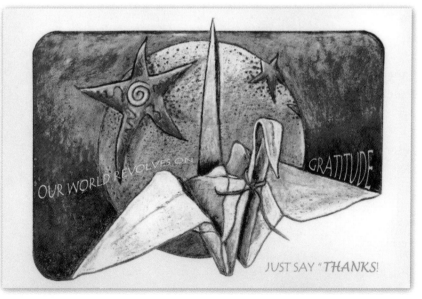

—Barbara Scavotto-Earley

CONNECT

Although it was impossible to track down everyone because many cards arrived anonymously with no return address, here are a few professional artists and community members (in order of appearance) who told me they would love to connect with you.

Mohammed Massoud Morsi
mindzoom.dk
P. 3, 32, 149, 189

Joe Galiette
galiettefusionphotoart.com
P. 9–10

Sara Drought Nebel
justplainart.com
P. 12, 41

Judith Barbour Osborne
jboart.com
P. 14–15, 121

Natalie Banker
www.nataliemakesart.com
P. 22

Noah Kaeser
noahkaeser.wordpress.com
P. 23

Betsy Devany
betsydevany.com
P. 30, 101

MJ Stevenson
mjstevensonart.blogspot.com
P. 33

Diana Lyn Cote
dianalyncote.com
P. 37, 46–47, 48–49, 56–57, 67, 86–87,
105, 112, 116, 132, 142, 151, 163, 169,
176–77, 191, 195, 198, 212

Keith Fox
keithfoxstudio.com
P. 38

Lon Cameron
portlandpalletworks.com
P. 43–44

Barbara Scavotto-Earley
scavottosculpture.com
P. 50–51, 227

Laurie Kammer
riseuplaurie.com
P. 69

Wendy Natter
wendystravelogue.blogspot.com
P. 75, 105, 155

Gale Simonson
galesimonson.com
P. 82

Lisa Sobolewski
lisasobolewski.com
P. 102, 107, 152, 196, 219

Dan Yagmin Jr.
danyagminjr.com
P. 103

Jill Butler
jillbutler.com
P. 104

Vladimir Shpitalnik
shpitalnik.com
P. 111–12, 210–11

Van Logan Franklin
vanloganfranklin.viewbook.com
P. 117

Mike Booth
riodeloso.com
P. 118

Christopher Zhang
chriszhangstudio.com
P. 119

Henrique de Sousa
newhorizonsbrazil.org
P. 127–28

Nancy Smith Worthen
magsarts.com
P. 141, 168

Ingrid Mathews
wildiris.zenfolio.com
P. 153

Evgeny Bam
vimeo.com/35140768
P. 202–3

David M. Miller
davidmillerart.com
P. 208

Adrien Broom
www.adrienbroom.com
P. 216

After looking at this card for weeks, I have realized that the thing I am most grateful for this season is,

THIS CARD!

It has forced me to give daily consideration to who, what and why, I am gratefull. As a result, I am going through life much more joyfully and with a greater appreciation of my self and those around me.

The Gratitude Trail at Hammonasset Beach State Park in the summer of 2013

Anne (AOK) Kubitsky

Because my last name is a bit of a mouthful, I often go by AOK. I'm a writer and artist with a background in biology and philosophy. Since The Look for the Good Project began, I have unexpectedly discovered love, strength, peace, abundance, insight, and a lighthearted laughter that I forgot I had. So, most of all, I am grateful to *you* for your interest in this project and the community that's forming around this one little question: What Makes YOU Grateful? I can't wait to see what happens next!

To join me, please visit:

lookforthegoodproject.org